RISK EFFICACY

Risk Efficacy

ALIA WU

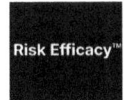

Copyright © 2026 by Alia Wu
All rights reserved. No part of this book may be reproduced in any manner whatsoever without written permission except in the case of brief quotations embodied in critical articles and reviews.
First Printing, 2026

CONTENTS

Series Introduction — 1

Introduction — 5

Part I: The Measurement Problem — 10

Chapter 1: What We Can't See — 11

Chapter 2: The Silent Components — 19

Part II: The Risk Efficacy Framework — 30

Chapter 3: The Calibration Gap — 31

Chapter 4: Informed Navigation — 41

Chapter 5: Resilience: From Adaptation to Recovery — 54

Chapter 6: Outcome Achievement – Beyond Results — 66

Chapter 7: The Integration of Pillars — 78

Part III: The New Infrastructure — 92

Chapter 8: From Theory to Practice — 93

Chapter 9: Building Measurement Systems 106

Chapter 10: Recognizing Merit in Uncertainty 118

Chapter 11: Cultivating a Culture of Risk Efficacy 132

Chapter 12: Scaling the Architecture 145

Chapter 13: The Future of Decision-Making 160

Appendix A: Risk Efficacy Assessment Tools 174
Appendix B: Implementation Resources 181
Appendix C: Key Research by Chapter 186
Appendix D: Glossary of Key Terms 192
Appendix E: Recommended Reading & Resources 194
Appendix F: Acknowledgments 196
Reference List 198
About the Author 213

Series Introduction

We live in societies that claim to be meritocracies. Organizations assert they promote the most capable people. Educational institutions maintain they admit the most talented students. Investment systems claim they fund the best ideas. Political systems proclaim they elevate the most qualified leaders.

These claims are largely false.

Not because people are deliberately dishonest, but because the infrastructure we use to identify, measure, and reward merit is fundamentally broken.

We've built elaborate systems for evaluating human capability that consistently measure the wrong things. They reward confidence over competence (Anderson et al., 2012), pedigree over performance, conformity over capability, visibility over value creation.

The result is a systematic misallocation of human potential on a massive scale. High performers get filtered out for not fitting subjective mental models of talent. Overconfident individuals get promoted into positions where their poor judgment creates expensive failures (Lovallo & Kahneman, 2003). Brilliant minds get overlooked for lacking the right credentials or networks.

This misallocation isn't merely unfair—though it certainly is that. It's profoundly inefficient. Organizations lose billions by promoting based on presence rather than decision-making capability. Societies squander their most valuable resource—human talent—because their measurement systems are biased toward easily observable traits rather than actual performance.

This inefficiency has reached an inflection point. The rapid adoption of artificial intelligence tools has fundamentally reshaped what counts as valuable judgment. The ability to synthesize information, identify relevant patterns, and iterate quickly through uncertainty now matters more than accumulated credentials and institutional pedigree.

The compounded productivity gap between organizations and societies that can identify and leverage this ability in their human capital and those that cannot will cost the latter more than money. This problem is becoming existential.

The Meritocracy Society Infrastructure Series exists to solve this problem systematically.

Each book addresses one critical piece of the infrastructure that determines who succeeds and who gets filtered out. Together, they provide a blueprint for rebuilding our talent systems so that merit—actual capability to create value and make good decisions—is what gets measured and rewarded.

This is not a series about aspiration or inspiration. It is not about helping individuals navigate broken systems, though that guidance appears where relevant.

This series is about redesigning the systems themselves.

The Infrastructure Problem

Infrastructure is invisible until it fails. You don't think about the bridge until it collapses. The power grid until it goes dark.

The same is true for talent infrastructure. The assessment frameworks, promotion systems, and credentialing mechanisms that determine who gets opportunities operate in the background, shaping outcomes without scrutiny. Until someone asks: are we actually promoting our best people?

When that question gets examined rigorously, the answer is almost always no.

Statistical analysis reveals that subjective assessments of "leadership potential" correlate weakly, if at all, with actual effectiveness (Kaiser et al., 2008). The credentials that open doors predict initial placement but not long-term performance. The networks that allocate resources are based on social proximity, not demonstrated capability.

This infrastructure evolved without intentional design. Organizations adopted subjective assessments because objective measurement was difficult. Educational institutions used simple metrics to process thousands of applications. These choices were understandable in their original contexts, but they've calcified into systems that actively prevent meritocracy.

Fixing this requires infrastructure replacement, not incremental reform. You cannot patch a broken bridge. You have to rebuild it.

This series provides the new systems.

Book One: Risk Efficacy

The first and most fundamental infrastructure problem is measurement. If you cannot accurately measure who makes good decisions under pressure, you cannot build a functioning meritocracy. Risk Efficacy provides an alternative framework, measuring decision-making capability through observable dimensions of informed navigation, calibration, resilience, and outcome achievement. This book establishes the theoretical foundation, introduces the framework, and provides an implementation toolkit.

Future Books in the Series

While this first volume establishes the measurement foundation, subsequent books will address other critical infrastructure challenges. The following volumes are planned:

- **Book Two** will examine how neurodivergent individuals are systematically filtered out by talent systems designed around

neurotypical norms, despite evidence of exceptional capability in pattern recognition and systematic thinking.
- **Book Three** will analyze how educational credentials function as gatekeeping mechanisms that increasingly measure access and resources rather than capability.
- **Book Four** will investigate how resources (venture capital, budgets, promotions) flow to those with existing networks and pitching skill rather than execution capability.
- **Book Five** will examine how broken feedback infrastructure prevents continued excellence even when capable individuals are identified.

How This Series Works

Each book follows a consistent structure:

- Part I: The Evidence documents the infrastructure problem.
- Part II: The Framework introduces the alternative.
- Part III: The Implementation provides tools for system change.

The ultimate goal is making meritocracy real rather than rhetorical. This requires replacing the infrastructure we use to identify, develop, and promote talent.

The work matters because talent is the primary constraint on human progress. The problems we face will be solved by capable people making good decisions under uncertainty. Our current infrastructure systematically prevents many of the most capable people from getting that opportunity.

We can do better. This series shows how.

Introduction

If you want to know who's good at something, look at what they've done. This seems straightforward enough. We do it all the time—in hiring, promotions, admissions. We look at outcomes: wins, revenues, grades, titles.

But here's the problem that becomes apparent to anyone who works in genuinely uncertain environments: outcomes are noisy signals. In fields where chance plays a significant role—which is to say, most interesting fields—the relationship between decision quality and outcomes is probabilistic, not deterministic. Good decisions can lead to bad outcomes. Bad decisions can lead to good outcomes (Baron & Hershey, 1988).

This problem is particularly acute in domains where risk is inherent and expertise is subtle: quantitative trading, trauma surgery, emergency response. Professionals in these fields learn to distinguish between the quality of a decision and the quality of its outcome. They know intimately: you can only control your process, not your results.

The same pattern appears at a systemic level. In 2010, a paper by Eugene Fama and Kenneth French in the Journal of Finance examined whether top hedge fund managers exhibited genuine skill or simply benefited from luck. The conclusion was sobering: for most, their performance was indistinguishable from random chance (Fama & French, 2010). The signal of skill was buried in the noise of randomness.

We see it everywhere: excellent surgeons have patients who die from unforeseeable complications. Brilliant products fail because of market timing. The better team doesn't always win.

We've developed specialized coping mechanisms. In finance, we talk about "process over outcomes." In medicine, we conduct morbidity and mortality conferences. In aviation, we investigate pilot error through systems analysis (Weick & Sutcliffe, 2007). But these are solutions for specialized domains. What about everywhere else?

Most organizations have no systematic way to distinguish between skill and luck. They promote based on results. They hire based on track records. They celebrate winners and avoid losers. And in doing so, they create systems that are good at recognizing luck but bad at recognizing skill.

The Measurement Problem

We like to think we live in a meritocracy—that the most skilled rise to the top. But a true meritocracy requires measurement infrastructure. You need ways to measure merit that actually track what matters.

In domains where performance is straightforward, we have reasonably good systems. To find the fastest sprinter, you hold a race. To find the best math student, you give a test.

But in domains where performance involves complex decision-making under uncertainty, our measurement infrastructure is primitive. We use proxies—outcomes, credentials, reputations—that are only loosely correlated with actual decision-making ability. And these proxies are systematically biased in predictable ways.

This isn't just an academic concern. When organizations can't accurately identify decision-making skill, they make poor choices about who leads, who gets resources, and who sets strategy. They promote people who are good at explaining outcomes rather than people who are good at creating them.

Worse, these faulty measurement systems create perverse incentives. If you get ahead by having good outcomes rather than by making good decisions, you'll optimize for outcomes—often at the expense of decision quality. You'll take credit for lucky breaks. You'll hide mistakes. You'll avoid reasonable risks. You'll focus on optics rather than substance (Kerr, 1975).

A Different Kind of Measurement

This book is an attempt to solve what you might call the merit recognition problem in uncertain environments. How do we identify true expertise when outcomes are unreliable guides?

The answer lies in measuring decision-making as a process. It requires looking at how people decide: how they gather information, how they handle uncertainty, how they execute, how they recover, and how well their confidence aligns with reality. I call this collection of measurable capacities Risk Efficacy.

The framework emerged from fifteen years of observation across multiple high-stakes domains, synthesized with research from cognitive neuroscience (Bechara et al., 1997), judgment and decision-making (Kahneman & Tversky, 1979; Tetlock & Gardner, 2015), and organizational psychology (Edmondson, 1999). It's grounded in evidence but designed for practical application.

The most interesting finding—and the one that gives this work its urgency—is that certain patterns of excellent decision-making are systematically misunderstood. We tend to recognize one pattern while undervaluing another.

The first pattern is what we might call bold clarity: decisive, confident, intuitive. This is the pattern we celebrate. When it succeeds, it looks like brilliance. When it fails, it looks like hubris.

The second pattern is calculated navigation: methodical, probabilistic, adaptive. This pattern involves explicit risk assessment, contingency planning, and constant updating. When it succeeds, it often looks like caution that happened to work out. When it fails, it looks like hesitation or indecision.

The problem isn't that one pattern is better—both can be excellent in the right context. The problem is that our recognition systems are biased toward the first pattern. We mistake confidence for competence, decisiveness for wisdom.

This bias has consequences. It means we systematically undervalue certain approaches to decision-making. And because these approaches aren't evenly distributed across populations—research suggests women, for example, are more likely to use deliberate, probabilistic approaches (Byrnes et al., 1999)—we systematically undervalue certain people.

What This Book Does

Risk Efficacy provides a way out of this trap. It measures decision-making capability through four observable dimensions:

1. Calibration: The ability to maintain confidence that accurately matches reality.
2. Informed Navigation: The ability to gather and integrate relevant information while explicitly accounting for uncertainty.
3. Resilience: The ability to execute with both proactive adaptation and effective recovery.
4. Outcome Achievement: The ability to achieve intended results consistently.

This book has three aims:

- To explain why our current methods of recognizing excellence often fail
- To provide a framework for measuring decision quality that works across domains
- To show how organizations can build better systems for identifying and developing true decision-making expertise

The book is structured in three parts:

- Part I: The Measurement Problem explores why our current approaches fail in uncertain environments.
- Part II: The Framework introduces the four components of Risk Efficacy and how to measure them.

- Part III: The New Infrastructure explores how organizations can implement Risk Efficacy measurement to build better systems for hiring, promotion, and strategy.

The work is necessarily incomplete—a framework rather than a finished system. But it's a start. And in domains where we currently judge by the roulette wheel rather than by the play, even a start represents progress.

We begin with the most fundamental question: what are we actually trying to measure when we try to identify good decision-makers? And why do we so often measure the wrong thing?

Part I: The Measurement Problem

Chapter 1: What We Can't See

The Visible and the Hidden

In the winter of 1995, a young derivatives trader at Barings Bank named Nick Leeson made a series of decisions that would ultimately destroy the 233-year-old institution. From the outside, as his risky bets initially paid off, he looked like a star—someone producing extraordinary returns. He was promoted, celebrated, given more responsibility. Only later would it become clear that what looked like skill was actually massive, hidden risk-taking.

The Barings collapse illustrates a fundamental problem in assessing decision-making: we often can't see the important parts. We see outcomes—profits, wins, successes. We don't see the risk exposures, the near-misses, the alternatives considered and rejected, the uncertainties that were acknowledged or ignored.

This problem isn't unique to finance. Consider:

- A CEO makes an acquisition that initially boosts the stock price. We celebrate her boldness. What we don't see is whether she properly assessed integration risks, whether she considered alternatives, whether the success was due to her decision or to favorable market conditions.
- A surgeon has excellent patient outcomes. We consider her skilled. What we don't see is whether she takes appropriate

risks with challenging cases or refers them out, whether her outcomes are due to her skill or to careful case selection.
- A product manager launches a feature that goes viral. We promote him. What we don't see is whether he understood why it succeeded, whether it was strategic or accidental, whether he can replicate the success.

In each case, the visible metric—the outcome—tells us something, but not enough. It's like judging a navigator by whether the ship reached port, without knowing whether they took the safe route or gambled through a storm.

The Research: Outcomes as Noisy Signals

The academic literature offers ample evidence that outcomes are poor measures of decision quality in uncertain environments.

In a classic 1977 study, Mahoney asked subjects to evaluate the quality of scientific research based on its outcomes. They presented identical methodologies but varied whether the results were positive or negative. Consistently, studies with positive results were rated as higher quality—even though the methodology was the same. The outcome biased the evaluation of process.

More recently, research on the "outcome bias" has shown that people judge decisions as better when they lead to good outcomes, even when the decision process is held constant (Baron & Hershey, 1988). This bias is remarkably resistant to correction—even when people are explicitly told to ignore outcomes and focus on process, they still can't completely do so.

In organizational contexts, the problem is compounded by what psychologists call "fundamental attribution error"—the tendency to attribute others' successes and failures to their character or abilities rather than to circumstances (Ross, 1977). When someone succeeds, we assume they're skilled. When they fail, we assume they're not. We discount the role of luck, context, and systemic factors.

This creates what the sociologist Robert Merton called a "self-fulfilling prophecy" in meritocratic systems (Merton, 1948). People who have early successes (whether from skill or luck) get more resources, more opportunities, and more attention, which makes further success more likely. Meanwhile, people who have early setbacks (whether from lack of skill or bad luck) get fewer resources and opportunities, making success less likely. Over time, the system amplifies initial differences, creating the illusion that the winners were always the most skilled.

The Two Types of Uncertainty

To understand why outcomes mislead us, it helps to distinguish between two types of uncertainty that decision-makers face:

Aleatory uncertainty—uncertainty due to randomness, to the inherent unpredictability of events. This is the "noise" in the system. In trading, it's market movements. In medicine, it's patient-specific responses. In product development, it's user behavior. Aleatory uncertainty cannot be reduced by better analysis; it can only be acknowledged and managed.

Epistemic uncertainty—uncertainty due to lack of knowledge. This is uncertainty that could, in principle, be reduced with better information, better models, or better analysis. It's the "unknown unknowns" that become "known unknowns" with effort.

Good decision-makers distinguish between these two types of uncertainty. They invest effort in reducing epistemic uncertainty (gathering information, building better models) while acknowledging and planning for aleatory uncertainty (building margins of safety, having contingency plans).

The problem with outcome-based evaluation is that it conflates the two. A good outcome might result from skillful reduction of epistemic uncertainty. Or it might result from favorable aleatory uncertainty (good luck). A bad outcome might result from poor handling of epistemic uncertainty. Or it might result from unfavorable aleatory uncertainty (bad luck).

Without visibility into the decision process, we can't tell which is which.

The Invisibility of Counterfactuals

Another reason outcomes mislead us is that we only see what happened, not what might have happened. Decision quality involves comparing the chosen path not just to what actually occurred, but to what would have occurred under alternative choices.

The trader who makes a risky bet and wins looks brilliant. But was it a good decision? That depends on the alternatives. If a safer bet would have produced nearly as much gain with far less risk, the risky bet was actually poor decision-making—it just happened to work out.

The surgeon who operates on a high-risk patient and succeeds looks heroic. But was it the right decision? That depends on what would have happened with conservative management. If the patient would have recovered nearly as well without surgery, the operation exposed them to unnecessary risk.

Psychologically, we're bad at thinking about counterfactuals—the paths not taken. Research shows that people have difficulty accurately imagining alternative scenarios, especially when the actual outcome is known (Roese, 1997). We're subject to "hindsight bias"—once we know what happened, it's hard to remember how uncertain things felt beforehand.

Good decision-makers, however, think explicitly about counterfactuals. They consider multiple scenarios. They assign probabilities. They make contingency plans. But this thinking is largely invisible to observers. All we see is the choice that was made and the outcome that occurred.

The Special Case of Near-Misses

Some of the most important information about decision quality comes from near-misses—situations where a bad outcome almost occurred but didn't.

The trader who takes excessive risk but gets bailed out by a market rally.

The surgeon who barely avoids a complication through quick intervention.

The racing driver who corrects an error just before it becomes catastrophic.

In outcome-based systems, these look like successes. The trader made money. The patient recovered. The race was won. But in process terms, they're often failures—or at least warnings. They reveal risk exposures, skill gaps, or system vulnerabilities that, under slightly different circumstances, would have led to disaster.

High-reliability organizations like aviation and nuclear power have developed systems to capture and learn from near-misses. They recognize that near-misses contain valuable information about decision quality that outcomes obscure. But most organizations lack such systems. They only count the disasters, not the near-disasters.

This creates what the sociologist Charles Perrow calls "normalization of deviance" (Perrow, 1984). When risky decisions repeatedly don't lead to bad outcomes, people start to believe the decisions aren't actually risky. They lower their standards. They accept more risk. Eventually, disaster strikes—not because anything changed in that moment, but because the system gradually drifted into danger.

The Measurement Challenge

All of this creates a measurement challenge: how do we assess decision quality when:

- Outcomes are noisy signals of quality
- We can't see the alternatives considered
- We can't distinguish between aleatory and epistemic uncertainty
- Near-misses look like successes
- Counterfactuals are invisible

The traditional answer has been to rely on credentials, reputation, and interviews—proxies that are themselves problematic. Credentials signal conformity to established paths more than decision-making ability. Reputation is vulnerable to the same outcome biases we've discussed. Interviews are notoriously poor predictors of performance, subject to all sorts of biases and limitations.

What we need is something more direct: a way to observe decision processes as they happen, or to reconstruct them afterward with enough fidelity to assess their quality.

That's what the risk efficacy framework attempts to provide. It offers a set of dimensions along which decision processes can be measured—dimensions that research suggests correlate with expertise across domains, but that are largely invisible in outcome-based assessment.

A Thought Experiment

Imagine two traders, Alice and Bob.

Alice makes 100 trades. For each trade, she:

- Researches the company thoroughly
- Considers multiple scenarios
- Calculates her position size based on her confidence level
- Sets clear stop-losses and profit targets
- Documents her reasoning beforehand

Bob also makes 100 trades. He:

- Goes on intuition
- Takes large positions
- Doesn't use stop-losses
- Doesn't document his reasoning

At the end of the year, Alice is up 12%. Bob is up 15%. Who's the better trader?

In most firms, Bob gets the bigger bonus. He produced better returns. But if we could see their processes, we might judge differently. Maybe Alice's process is sustainable and replicable. Maybe Bob took reckless risks that happened to pay off. Maybe Alice's 12% represents skill while Bob's 15% represents luck.

The problem is that in most organizations, we can't see their processes. We only see their results. And so we reward Bob, promote Bob, give Bob more capital to manage. Until, eventually, his luck runs out.

This isn't just a trading problem. It's a problem anywhere decisions are made under uncertainty. And it's a problem the risk efficacy framework aims to solve.

Toward Better Measurement

The chapters that follow will build a framework for measuring what we currently can't see. They'll propose that decision quality can be assessed along four dimensions:

1. **Calibration**—How well does someone's confidence match their accuracy?
2. **Informed Navigation**—How thoroughly and effectively does someone gather and process relevant information while explicitly accounting for uncertainty?
3. **Resilience**—How do they implement decisions with both proactive adaptation and effective recovery when things go wrong?
4. **Outcome Achievement**—How consistently do they achieve intended results?

These dimensions aren't exhaustive, but they capture important aspects of decision quality that outcomes obscure. They're based on research into expertise across domains. And they're measurable—not perfectly, but meaningfully.

More importantly, they help us distinguish between different patterns of excellence. The bold, intuitive decision-maker and the methodical, analytical decision-maker might score differently on these dimensions, but both could score highly in different ways. The framework gives us a language to recognize excellence in multiple forms, rather than celebrating one pattern while misunderstanding another.

That's the goal: to build measurement infrastructure that recognizes true expertise, whatever form it takes. To create systems where the Alice's of the world get recognized alongside the Bob's—not because we have quotas or preferences, but because we're actually measuring what matters.

We begin with the first dimension: how well our confidence matches reality.

Chapter 2: The Silent Components

What Isn't in the Ledger

In 2011, a team of neuroscientists published a study that changed how we think about decision-making under pressure. They placed chess masters in an fMRI scanner while they evaluated complex positions (Bilalić et al., 2011). The surprising finding wasn't what the masters thought about, but what they didn't have to think about. Expert players showed less activation in the prefrontal cortex—the region associated with deliberate, effortful reasoning—and more in pattern recognition networks. Their expertise had become, in a neurological sense, invisible.

This invisibility of expertise presents the central measurement problem of our time. In domains where decisions matter most, the most important components often leave no trace. A trader's risk calculation, a surgeon's differential diagnosis, a racing driver's situation awareness—these happen internally, leaving only the final decision visible. And when we try to measure what we can't see, we end up measuring what we can: outcomes, credentials, confidence. These become our proxies, our stand-ins for something that remains fundamentally unobserved.

The problem with proxies is that they drift. Confidence becomes separated from competence. Credentials become separated from capability. Outcomes become separated from quality. And before long, we're not measuring what matters at all.

The Research: When Process Becomes Invisible

Studies across domains reveal a consistent pattern: as expertise develops, the decision process becomes less visible, even to the decision-maker themselves.

In a landmark 1996 study, Charness and colleagues examined chess masters. When asked to verbalize their thinking during a game, experts gave less detailed explanations than intermediate players, not because they knew less, but because more of their processing had become automatic (Charness et al., *Cognitive Psychology*, 1996). What looked like intuition from the outside was actually compressed expertise—years of pattern recognition packed into milliseconds.

Similarly, research on medical diagnosis shows that experts often can't articulate exactly how they arrive at correct diagnoses (Norman et al., *Academic Medicine*, 2007). They know the answer feels right, but the steps have become procedural. This creates what cognitive scientists call the "expertise paradox": the more expert someone becomes, the harder it is for them—and for observers—to see how they make decisions.

This paradox has profound implications for merit recognition. If we can't see the decision process, and experts can't articulate it, how do we know who's actually good? How do we distinguish between genuine expertise and lucky guessing?

The Components We Miss

Based on ten years of observation across high-stakes domains, I've identified four silent components of decision-making that traditional measurement systems consistently miss:

1. The Quality of Information Integration

Not all information is created equal. The key isn't how much information someone has, but how well they integrate it—how they weigh conflicting signals, how they update their beliefs with new evidence, how they distinguish signal from noise.

In a 2009 study, Fenton-O'Creevy and colleagues examined traders in investment banks (*Organization Science*, 2009). They found that the most successful traders weren't those with the most information, but those with the best filters. They knew what to ignore. They updated their views quickly when presented with contradictory evidence. They maintained what the researchers called "constructive doubt"—enough confidence to act, but enough uncertainty to keep learning.

Yet in most organizations, we measure information gathering by volume—how many reports someone reads, how many meetings they attend—not by quality. We reward people for being informed, not for being discerning.

2. The Handling of Uncertainty

Uncertainty comes in layers. There's the uncertainty you acknowledge, the uncertainty you quantify, and the uncertainty you plan for. Most measurement systems capture only the first, if that.

Consider two surgeons presented with the same complex case. The first says: "I'm 95% confident we should operate." The second says: "Given the evidence, I estimate a 70% chance that surgery is the best option. There's a 20% chance that conservative management would be better, and a 10% chance we're missing something critical. I'd like to order one more test to reduce that last uncertainty, and if we proceed, we should have contingency plans A, B, and C ready."

In outcome-based systems, both surgeons might be credited equally if the surgery succeeds. But their approaches to uncertainty are fundamentally different. The second surgeon's thinking is more sophisticated, more probabilistic, more robust. Yet it's also less confident-sounding, less decisive, less leaderly by conventional standards.

Research by Brescoll (2012) shows that women are more likely to express uncertainty in this probabilistic way, while men are more likely to express confidence even when uncertain. This creates what I've come to call the "confidence-competence mismatch": systems that reward confidence mistake it for competence, systematically favoring one style over another.

3. The Quality of Alternatives Considered

The quality of a decision cannot be judged by the path taken alone. It must be judged against the paths not taken—the alternatives that were considered and rejected.

In a remarkable study of expert versus novice decision-makers, Klein and colleagues (*Human Factors*, 1995) found that experts don't just choose better options; they consider better options to begin with. When presented with a complex scenario, experts immediately generate several plausible courses of action, then systematically eliminate the weakest. Novices, by contrast, often fixate on the first reasonable option they encounter.

This process of generating and evaluating alternatives is almost entirely invisible. All we see is the final choice. A decision-maker who considers three excellent alternatives and chooses the best looks identical to one who considers one mediocre alternative and chooses it.

4. The Quality of Adaptation

No decision survives contact with reality unchanged. The real test of decision quality isn't in the initial choice, but in how someone adapts as circumstances evolve.

In high-stakes environments, this adaptive capacity is often the difference between success and failure. The trader who adjusts position sizes as volatility changes. The surgeon who modifies the approach when unexpected anatomy appears. The racing driver who changes course when weather deteriorates.

Yet adaptation is particularly difficult to measure because it happens in real time, often under pressure. And it's frequently misinterpreted: the decision-maker who changes course is seen as uncertain or indecisive, while the one who sticks to the original plan is seen as confident and committed—even when sticking to the plan is the wrong choice.

Research on adaptive expertise highlights this tension (Hatano & Inagaki, 1986). Adaptive experts know when to follow procedures and when to innovate. They're comfortable with uncertainty. They see exceptions not as annoyances but as information. Yet this very adaptability can make them seem less expert by traditional measures—less consistent, less predictable, less adherent to protocol.

The Measurement Consequences

When we miss these silent components, our measurement systems develop systematic biases:

We favor decisive over deliberate. Decisiveness is visible; deliberation is not. Someone who makes quick decisions looks more confident, more leaderly. Someone who takes time to consider options looks hesitant, uncertain.

We favor consistent over adaptive. Consistency is easy to measure; adaptation is not. Someone who sticks to their plan looks committed. Someone who changes course looks wishy-washy.

We favor certain over probabilistic. Certainty is clear; probabilistic thinking is messy. Someone who says "This will work" sounds more convincing than someone who says "This has an 80% chance of working, and here's what we do in the other 20% of cases."

We favor action over contemplation. Action produces measurable results; contemplation produces only thoughts. Someone who acts quickly gets credit for initiative. Someone who thinks first gets labeled as slow.

These biases aren't just measurement errors; they're selection errors. They systematically favor one approach to decision-making over others. And because these approaches aren't evenly distributed across populations—research consistently shows gender differences in risk communication, for example (Byrnes et al., *Psychological Bulletin*, 1999)—they systematically favor certain people over others.

The High Cost of Missing Signals

The consequences of missing these silent components are most visible in fields where decisions have immediate, measurable consequences.

In quantitative trading, I've seen firms promote traders based on returns alone, only to discover—sometimes catastrophically—that their star performers were taking hidden risks, failing to properly hedge, or getting lucky in ways that wouldn't repeat. The traders who produced steady, risk-adjusted returns often went unrecognized because their approach looked conservative rather than brilliant.

In medicine, studies show that surgeons with the best outcomes aren't always the ones who take the most challenging cases (Birkmeyer et al., *New England Journal of Medicine*, 2003). Some achieve excellent outcomes through careful patient selection—operating only when success is likely. Others achieve similar outcomes by taking on riskier cases and managing the complexity skillfully. Outcome measures alone can't distinguish between these approaches, yet they represent fundamentally different types of expertise.

In emergency response, research on incident commanders shows that the most effective leaders aren't necessarily the most decisive (Klein, *Sources of Power*, 1998). They're the ones who maintain situation awareness, who continuously update their assessment, who adapt their plans as new information emerges. Yet in training and evaluation, decisiveness is often emphasized over adaptability.

Making the Invisible Visible

The challenge, then, is to develop measurement systems that capture these silent components—not perfectly, but meaningfully. Systems that can distinguish between:

- Information gathering and information integration
- Confidence and calibrated confidence
- Decisiveness and deliberation
- Consistency and appropriate adaptation

The risk efficacy framework represents one attempt to solve this measurement problem. It starts from a simple premise: if we can't observe decision processes directly, we can observe their traces. We can measure what people pay attention to, how they update their beliefs, how they handle surprises, how their confidence matches their accuracy.

The framework focuses on four dimensions:

- **1. Calibration** – How well does confidence match reality over time
- **2. Informed Navigation** – How thoroughly information is gathered and integrated with explicit uncertainty accounting
- **3. Resilience** – How effectively decisions are executed with both adaptation planning and recovery capability
- **4. Outcome Achievement** – How consistently intended results are achieved

Each dimension can be measured through observable behaviors: what questions people ask, how they respond to new information, how they explain their reasoning, how they track predictions versus outcomes.

A New Way of Seeing

Consider two portfolio managers, Maya and Ben. Both have produced 15% annual returns over five years.

Traditional evaluation would look at their returns, maybe adjust for risk using standard metrics, and conclude they're equally skilled. But a closer examination reveals different patterns:

Maya's returns come from steady, consistent performance. She outperforms in down markets, underperforms slightly in up markets. When asked about her approach, she talks about risk management first, returns second. She keeps a decision journal where she records her reasoning for each trade, then reviews what actually happened. She can point to specific instances where she changed her mind based on new evidence.

Ben's returns are more volatile. He has spectacular years and mediocre ones. He attributes his success to "conviction" and "sticking to his guns." He's confident in his predictions, often expressing near-certainty. His performance reviews praise his "decisiveness" and "willingness to take bold positions."

Who's the better portfolio manager?

By traditional measures, they're equal. But by risk efficacy measures, we might see things differently. Maya shows better calibration—her confidence matches her accuracy. She demonstrates informed navigation—she gathers diverse information and acknowledges uncertainties. She shows resilience—she adapts when evidence warrants.

Ben, for all his confidence, might be overconfident. His "conviction" might be stubbornness. His "decisiveness" might be failure to update.

The problem isn't that one approach is always better. In some market conditions, Ben's approach might outperform. The problem is that our measurement systems can't distinguish between the approaches at all. We see only the outcomes, not the processes that produced them.

Toward Better Measurement

Developing measurement systems that capture these silent components requires a fundamental shift: from measuring what's easy to measure toward measuring what matters.

It requires:

- **Process transparency** – Creating ways for decision-makers to make their thinking visible
- **Prediction tracking** – Comparing what people expect to happen with what actually happens
- **Reasoning documentation** – Capturing the why behind decisions, not just the what
- **Adaptation measurement** – Tracking how decisions evolve as circumstances change

These aren't radical ideas. In some domains, they're already standard practice. In aviation, pilots use checklists not because they don't know what to do, but to make their thinking visible and verifiable. In medicine, morbidity and mortality conferences examine decision processes, not just outcomes. In high-reliability organizations, near-misses are investigated as thoroughly as failures.

What's radical is applying these principles beyond specialized domains—to business, to education, to all the places where decisions matter but measurement is primitive.

The Path Forward

The silent components of decision-making will never be fully visible. Some aspects of expertise will always remain internal, intuitive, and tacit. But we can do better than we're doing now. We can develop measurement systems that capture more of what matters, that distinguish between different types of excellence, that recognize expertise in all its forms.

The first step is acknowledging what we're missing. The second is building systems to capture it. The chapters that follow will explore both.

Reflection Questions:

- 1. Think of someone you consider an expert in your field. What aspects of their decision-making are visible? What aspects remain hidden?
- 2. Consider your own decision-making. What silent components would be most valuable to make visible? What would you learn from seeing them?
- 3. What measurement systems in your organization capture silent components well? Which capture them poorly?

Exercise: The Decision Autopsy (Revisited)

Choose a past decision where the outcome is known. This time, focus not on what you decided, but on:

- 4. What information did you integrate? What did you ignore?
- 5. How did you handle uncertainty? Did you quantify it? Plan for it?
- 6. What alternatives did you consider? How did you evaluate them?
- 7. How did you adapt as circumstances changed?

Then ask: If you had to make this decision again with the same information, what would you do differently in your process (not your choice)?

Practice: Making Thinking Visible

For one week, practice making one silent component visible each day:

- Monday: Document three uncertainties in a decision you're facing

- Tuesday: List the alternatives you considered for a choice, and why you rejected them
- Wednesday: Track how you update your beliefs when presented with new information
- Thursday: Note how you adapt a plan when circumstances change
- Friday: Record your confidence level in a prediction, then track what actually happens

At the end of the week, review what you've learned about your own decision process.

Part II: The Risk Efficacy Framework

Chapter 3: The Calibration Gap

When Confidence Divorces Competence
In the late 1990s, a series of experiments revealed something unsettling about expert judgment. Researchers asked clinical psychologists to make diagnostic predictions about patients, then measured how often those predictions proved correct. The results, published by the *American Psychological Association (Garb 1998)*, showed something counterintuitive: as clinicians gained more experience, their confidence increased, but their accuracy did not. Their certainty grew while their correctness remained stagnant.

This phenomenon—the growing gap between confidence and accuracy—appears across domains. In finance, traders become more certain of their predictions without becoming more accurate (Barber & Odean, 2001). In medicine, experienced physicians show greater confidence in diagnoses without improved correctness (Berner & Graber, 2008). In business, seasoned executives express greater certainty about strategic decisions without better outcomes (Lovallo & Kahneman, 2003).

Why does this happen? And why does it matter for recognizing true expertise?

The Research: The Illusion of Validity
The calibration gap emerges from what psychologist Daniel Kahneman calls the "illusion of validity"—the unwarranted confidence we

have in our judgments, particularly when we have consistent information that appears to tell a coherent story (Kahneman, 2011).

In one telling study, researchers asked students and professional stock forecasters to predict corporate earnings (Andreassen, 1990). Both groups received the same information. The professionals expressed much higher confidence in their predictions, yet their accuracy was no better than the students'. The professionals' experience gave them the illusion of understanding—a sense that they could see patterns and make predictions—without actually improving their predictive power.

This illusion becomes particularly pronounced in what psychologist Philip Tetlock calls "hedgehog" thinkers—those who know one big thing, apply it everywhere, and express high confidence in their predictions (Tetlock, 2005). By contrast, "fox" thinkers—who know many small things, synthesize from multiple sources, and express appropriate uncertainty—often have better calibration but lower perceived confidence.

The problem for merit recognition systems is straightforward: we mistake confidence for competence. The hedgehog sounds more expert, even when the fox performs better.

Two Types of Confidence

To understand the calibration gap, we must distinguish between two fundamentally different types of confidence:

Epistemic confidence – Confidence based on knowledge, evidence, and reasoning. This confidence grows as understanding deepens and evidence accumulates. It's grounded in reality. When someone with high epistemic confidence says "I'm sure," they mean "The evidence strongly supports this conclusion."

Social confidence – Confidence expressed for social reasons: to persuade, to lead, to avoid appearing weak. This confidence may or may not align with actual knowledge. When someone with high social confidence says "I'm sure," they often mean "I want you to believe I'm sure."

Both types serve purposes. Social confidence can mobilize teams, secure resources, and drive action. Epistemic confidence represents genuine understanding. The trouble begins when systems reward one while needing the other—or when they can't tell the difference.

Research by Anderson and colleagues (*Psychological Science*, 2012) shows that in group settings, individuals who express higher confidence gain more influence, regardless of their actual expertise. The confident voice carries further than the calibrated one. This creates what organizational psychologists call "confidence bias"—the systematic advantage given to those who express certainty, independent of their accuracy.

The Neuroscience of Certainty

Recent neuroscience research helps explain why confidence and accuracy can diverge. Studies using fMRI show that feelings of certainty and actual knowledge are processed in partially separate neural pathways (Fleming et al., 2012).

When we feel confident about a decision, activity increases in the prefrontal cortex and anterior cingulate—regions involved in metacognition (thinking about thinking). But this confidence signal doesn't always correlate with activity in regions associated with factual knowledge or pattern recognition.

Even more intriguing: the neurotransmitter dopamine appears to play a role in confidence independent of accuracy (Lak et al., 2014). Higher dopamine levels correlate with greater confidence, not necessarily greater correctness. This may explain why certain personalities or states (mania, for example) feature high confidence without corresponding accuracy.

From an evolutionary perspective, this makes sense. In many ancestral environments, decisive leadership—even if occasionally wrong—may have been more valuable than perfectly calibrated hesitation. But in modern complex systems, miscalibrated confidence has different costs.

The Measurement Problem, Again

The calibration gap creates a fundamental measurement problem: how do we distinguish between well-earned confidence and empty certainty?

Traditional systems fail at this distinction. They measure confidence through self-report, presentation style, or decisiveness—all of which capture social confidence more reliably than epistemic confidence. They reward those who speak with certainty, who make bold predictions, who never say "I don't know."

This creates systematic misvaluation. Consider two data scientists:

Alex consistently says things like: "Based on the available data, there's approximately a 75% chance this model will improve accuracy by 3-5 percentage points. The key uncertainty is whether the training data represents production conditions. I recommend a phased rollout so we can monitor performance and adjust."

Jordan says: "This model will definitely improve accuracy by at least 5%. I've built dozens of models like this. Trust me."

In many organizations, Jordan gets promoted. Jordan sounds like a leader. Alex sounds like an academic. Yet over time, Alex's predictions prove more accurate. Alex understands uncertainty. Jordan ignores it.

Gender and Calibration

Research reveals particularly troubling patterns around gender and confidence calibration.

Multiple studies show that women tend to be better calibrated than men—their confidence more closely matches their accuracy (Lundeberg et al., 1994). Women are more likely to express uncertainty appropriately, to acknowledge what they don't know, to give probabilistic rather than definitive answers.

Yet this very calibration often gets penalized. In performance reviews, women receive more feedback about needing to be "more confident," "more decisive," "more authoritative" (Correll, 2017). Their appropriate uncertainty gets interpreted as lack of confidence, which gets interpreted as lack of competence.

The reverse happens for men. Overconfidence gets interpreted as confidence, which gets interpreted as competence. A man who expresses 90% confidence while being right 70% of the time gets promoted. A woman who expresses 70% confidence while being right 70% of the time gets told to work on her confidence.

This creates what sociologist Cecilia Ridgeway calls "the confidence gap that isn't a competence gap" (Ridgeway, 2014). The gap isn't in actual ability, but in how ability gets expressed and interpreted.

Calibration Across Domains

Different fields handle calibration differently, offering lessons for merit recognition systems.

Weather forecasting stands out as a domain where calibration is explicitly measured and valued. Meteorologists don't just predict rain or sun; they predict probabilities: "60% chance of precipitation." Their performance is evaluated not just on whether it rained, but on whether their probabilities matched reality. A forecaster who predicts 60% and it rains 60% of the time is perfectly calibrated, regardless of whether it rains on any particular day.

This probabilistic approach changes everything. It makes uncertainty visible and measurable. It rewards accurate assessment rather than lucky guessing. And research shows that with proper training and feedback, forecasters can achieve remarkable calibration (Murphy & Winkler, 1977).

Professional poker offers another example. Successful poker players think explicitly in probabilities. They calculate pot odds, estimate opponents' hand ranges, and make decisions based on expected value. Their confidence is quantified: "I'm 70% sure I have the best hand, so calling has positive expected value."

Poker also illustrates the difference between results-oriented thinking and process-oriented thinking. A player can make the mathematically correct decision and still lose the hand. Over time, good decisions lead to good results, but any single hand involves significant luck.

Emergency medicine represents a domain where calibration matters but is hard to measure. Physicians must make rapid decisions with incomplete information. The best maintain "calibrated urgency"—they act decisively while acknowledging uncertainty, gathering additional information when possible, and adjusting as new data emerges (Croskerry, 2009).

Research on diagnostic error shows that miscalibration contributes significantly to mistakes. Overconfident physicians fail to consider alternative diagnoses. Underconfident physicians order unnecessary tests or hesitate when action is needed.

Measuring Calibration

The risk efficacy framework proposes concrete ways to measure calibration:

- **Prediction tracking** – Have individuals make probabilistic predictions, then track outcomes. Calculate calibration scores: how often events they gave X% probability actually occurred.
- **Confidence intervals** – Ask for estimates with confidence intervals ("I'm 90% confident the value is between A and B"). Measure how often the true value falls within their intervals.
- **Post-decision reviews** – After decisions, ask: "How confident were you in this decision at the time?" Compare with outcomes.
- **Knowledge calibration** – Test factual knowledge, but also ask for confidence in each answer. Calculate the relationship between confidence and accuracy.

These measures don't capture everything about decision quality, but they capture something important: the relationship between what someone believes and what's actually true.

The Organizational Challenge

Implementing calibration measurement in organizations requires cultural shifts:

From certainty to probability – Organizations must learn to value probabilistic thinking. This means celebrating someone who says "There's an 80% chance this will work" rather than only rewarding those who say "This will work."

From decisiveness to appropriate speed – Not all decisions require the same speed. Some benefit from rapid action; others benefit from deliberate consideration. Organizations need to distinguish between appropriate deliberation and problematic delay.

From confidence to calibrated confidence – Performance reviews should evaluate whether confidence is justified, not just whether confidence is expressed.

From individual to system calibration – Organizations themselves can be miscalibrated. They can be overconfident about strategies, underconfident about innovations, systematically biased in their assessments. Measuring organizational calibration—how well the organization's collective confidence matches reality—is equally important.

Case Study: Bridgewater Associates

The investment firm Bridgewater Associates offers a provocative example of attempting to measure and improve calibration. Founder Ray Dalio implemented a system called "baseball cards" that rates employees on various attributes, including their "believability"—essentially, how well-calibrated they are (Dalio, 2017).

Employees who consistently make accurate predictions gain higher believability scores. Their opinions carry more weight in decisions. Those with poor calibration scores have less influence, regardless of their seniority or confidence.

The system isn't perfect—it has been criticized for creating a stressful culture—but it represents a serious attempt to solve the calibration measurement problem. It recognizes that in an uncertain world, knowing who to listen to matters as much as knowing what to do.

Toward Better Calibration

Improving calibration—both individual and organizational—requires specific practices:

Keep prediction journals – Record predictions, confidence levels, and outcomes. Review regularly to identify patterns of over- or under-confidence.

Practice probabilistic thinking – Express judgments numerically: "I'm 70% confident" rather than "pretty sure."

Seek disconfirming evidence – Actively look for information that might prove you wrong. This counters confirmation bias and improves calibration.

Use premortems – Before decisions, imagine they've failed. Ask: "What might cause this failure?" This surfaces overconfidence.

Create calibration-friendly environments – Reward appropriate uncertainty. Don't punish people for saying "I don't know" when they don't know.

Implement prediction markets – Allow groups to bet on outcomes. Prediction markets often yield well-calibrated probabilities by aggregating diverse opinions (Wolfers & Zitzewitz, 2004).

The Calibration Premium

Organizations that solve the calibration measurement problem gain what we might call a "calibration premium"—the advantage of seeing reality more clearly.

They make better decisions because they weigh opinions appropriately. They avoid disasters because they don't follow overconfident leaders off cliffs. They innovate more effectively because they accurately assess risks and opportunities.

Perhaps most importantly, they recognize true expertise wherever it appears—not just in those who sound confident, but in those who are right.

The Way Forward

The calibration gap represents one of the most persistent and damaging failures in merit recognition. We reward certainty over accuracy, confidence over competence, decisiveness over wisdom.

Closing this gap requires measurement systems that capture what we've traditionally missed: the relationship between belief and reality. It requires valuing probabilistic thinking in a world that prefers definitive answers. It requires creating spaces where appropriate uncertainty isn't punished but respected.

The next chapter will explore how we might build such systems—not just for calibration, but for all the silent components of decision quality. We'll examine what happens when we make the invisible visible, when we measure what matters rather than what's convenient.

Reflection Questions:

- 8. Think of someone in your organization who is well-calibrated. How are they perceived? Are they rewarded for their calibration or penalized for their uncertainty?
- 9. Consider your own calibration. Are there domains where you're consistently overconfident? Underconfident? What might explain these patterns?
- 10. What would change in your organization if calibration were measured and rewarded?

Exercise: Calibration Training

For one month, practice making and tracking probabilistic predictions:

- 11. Each day, make 3-5 predictions about events in your work or life. Assign each a probability (e.g., "70% chance the meeting will end on time").
- 12. Record your predictions and confidence levels.
- 13. When outcomes are known, record what happened.

- 14. At month's end, calculate:

  - What percentage of events you gave X% probability actually occurred
  - How often you were overconfident (assigned >50% probability to something that didn't happen)
  - How often you were underconfident (assigned <50% probability to something that did happen)

Practice: The Confidence Audit

Review recent decisions or statements you've made. For each, ask:

- 15. How confident was I in this at the time?
- 16. What evidence supported that confidence level?
- 17. What uncertainties did I acknowledge? What did I ignore?
- 18. How might I have expressed this confidence more accurately?

Then consider: If you had to assign a numerical probability to your confidence at the time, what would it have been? How does that compare with what you actually expressed?

Chapter 4: Informed Navigation

The Art of Knowing What Matters

In 2011, a team of neuroscientists at University College London conducted a study that would change how we think about expert decision-making. They placed chess masters and novices in fMRI scanners and watched their brains as they evaluated chess positions (Bilalić et al., *Cerebral Cortex*, 2011). The masters weren't just thinking harder or accessing more information. They were thinking differently. Their brains showed efficient activation in the temporal lobe—the region associated with pattern recognition—while novices showed scattered activation across multiple regions. The experts weren't processing more information; they were processing better information.

This finding points to the heart of informed navigation: the ability to distinguish signal from noise, to extract meaning from data, to build coherent understanding from disparate pieces, all while maintaining explicit awareness of what remains unknown. In high-stakes environments, this capacity separates exceptional decision-makers from merely competent ones. Yet it remains largely invisible to traditional measurement systems.

The Research: How Experts See Differently

Studies across domains reveal consistent patterns in how experts navigate information and uncertainty:

In medicine, research shows that expert diagnosticians don't gather more information than novices; they gather different information (Norman et al., *Advances in Health Sciences Education*, 2007). When presented with a complex case, novices tend to collect exhaustive lists of symptoms and test results. Experts, by contrast, quickly form initial hypotheses and then seek specific information to confirm or refute them. They practice what cognitive scientists call "hypothesis-driven information gathering"—a focused, efficient approach that minimizes irrelevant data.

In finance, a study of successful portfolio managers found that they spend less time consuming market information than their less successful peers (Fenton-O'Creevy et al., *Organization Science*, 2011). Instead, they focus on understanding structural factors, long-term trends, and valuation principles. They filter out daily noise to concentrate on meaningful signals. Their advantage isn't in having more information but in having better filters and more explicit uncertainty mapping.

In firefighting, research on command decision-making shows that experts don't process all available information (Klein, *Sources of Power*, 1998). They use what psychologist Gary Klein calls "recognition-primed decision-making": they quickly recognize patterns based on experience, then mentally simulate potential actions to see which feels right. This process integrates information not through conscious analysis but through pattern matching and mental simulation, while maintaining awareness of what they don't know about the evolving situation.

These studies point to a counterintuitive truth: better decision-makers often consider less information, not more. Their skill lies in knowing what to ignore, what to prioritize, and what uncertainties to track explicitly.

The Signal-to-Noise Problem

The fundamental challenge of informed navigation is the signal-to-noise ratio—the proportion of meaningful information to irrelevant data. In most modern environments, this ratio is declining rapidly.

Consider these statistics:

- The average professional receives 120+ emails daily (Radicati Group, 2023)
- There are over 2.5 quintillion bytes of data created daily (DOMO, 2023)
- The number of scientific papers published doubles every 9-15 years (Bornmann & Mutz, 2015)

This explosion of information creates what psychologist Daniel Levitin calls "cognitive overload"—the point at which our ability to process information breaks down (Levitin, *The Organized Mind*, 2014). When overloaded, we make poorer decisions, experience greater stress, and become less creative.

Research on information overload shows predictable effects:

- Decision quality declines beyond a certain information threshold (O'Reilly, 1980)
- People become more likely to rely on heuristics and biases (Malhotra, 1982)
- Stress hormones like cortisol increase, impairing prefrontal cortex function (Armstrong, 2019)

The most effective decision-makers develop strategies to manage this overload. They create what computer scientists call "lossy compression"—intentionally discarding less important information to preserve what matters most, while maintaining explicit track of what they're choosing to ignore and why.

The Components of Informed Navigation

Based on research across domains, I've identified four key components of effective informed navigation:

1. Source Diversity and Breadth

Not all information sources are created equal. Homogeneous information—even if abundant—leads to narrow understanding. Research on "echo chambers" and "filter bubbles" shows the dangers of information homogeneity (Pariser, *The Filter Bubble*, 2011). When people only consume information that aligns with their existing beliefs, their understanding becomes distorted. They become overconfident in their views and unable to anticipate alternative perspectives.

By contrast, navigating diverse information sources:

- Reduces overconfidence (Koriat et al., *Psychological Review*, 1980)
- Improves prediction accuracy (Surowiecki, *The Wisdom of Crowds*, 2004)
- Increases innovation (Page, *The Difference*, 2007)

The challenge is that seeking diverse information feels uncomfortable. It creates cognitive dissonance. It requires holding conflicting ideas simultaneously. But this very discomfort is often a sign of effective navigation.

Effective navigators consult multiple types of sources: quantitative data, expert opinion, frontline observations, historical patterns, and contrarian perspectives. They look outside their immediate team or domain. They recognize that the most valuable insights often come from unexpected places.

2. Signal-to-Noise Filtration

Not all filters are created equal. Poor filters discard valuable information while retaining noise. Excellent filters do the opposite.

Research on expert-novice differences in radiology provides a striking example (Kundel et al., *Radiology*, 2007). When expert radiologists examine X-rays, their eyes don't scan the entire image systematically. Instead, they make rapid saccades to areas most likely to contain abnormalities. Their visual system has learned where to look—and equally importantly, where not to look.

This filtering capacity develops through deliberate practice with feedback. It's what separates the chess master who immediately sees the critical squares from the novice who scans the entire board. It's what allows the experienced trader to ignore 99% of market data while focusing on the 1% that matters.

But filtration alone isn't enough. The best navigators maintain awareness of what they're filtering out. They can articulate why certain information was deemed irrelevant and could explain what would cause them to reconsider that judgment.

3. Uncertainty Accounting

This is the critical differentiator that separates informed navigation from mere information gathering. Before a commitment is made, how many key unknowns were explicitly identified and documented? Of those, how many were actively reduced or resolved before proceeding?

Research shows that explicit uncertainty acknowledgement improves decision quality across domains. In medicine, physicians who explicitly list diagnostic uncertainties make fewer errors (Berner & Graber, 2008). In finance, traders who quantify their uncertainties achieve better risk-adjusted returns (Fenton-O'Creevy et al., 2011).

The very act of maintaining a "known unknowns" ledger is a hallmark of intellectual honesty and calculated risk-taking. It represents the difference between saying "I don't know" (which traditional systems punish) and saying "Here are the five things I don't know, here's how I'm addressing each, and here's how I'll manage the residual uncertainty" (which should be rewarded but rarely is).

4. Synthesis and Complexity Management

Integration isn't just about filtering; it's about connecting. Synthesis is the ability to combine disparate pieces of information into coherent understanding while maintaining awareness of the system's complexity.

Neuroscience research shows that synthesis involves distinct brain regions. The default mode network—active when we're not focused on external tasks—plays a crucial role in making connections between seemingly unrelated concepts (Buckner et al., *Annals of the New York Academy of Sciences*, 2008). This network is more active in experienced decision-makers when they're considering complex problems.

Synthesis capacity explains why some people can take information from multiple domains and generate novel insights. It's what allows a physician to connect seemingly unrelated symptoms into a unified diagnosis. It's what enables a strategist to see how technological, social, and economic trends intersect to create new opportunities.

But synthesis must be paired with complexity awareness. Effective navigators don't oversimplify; they acknowledge complexity while finding patterns within it. They create mental models that are both comprehensive and comprehensible.

The Measurement Challenge

Traditional measurement systems capture informed navigation poorly:

They measure quantity over quality. Performance metrics often count hours spent researching, documents read, or data points collected. But they rarely assess whether the right information was gathered or whether uncertainties were properly accounted for.

They reward visible activity over invisible synthesis. The person who produces detailed reports gets credit for "thoroughness." The person who spends time thinking deeply about a problem may appear to be doing nothing.

They favor speed over navigation. Quick responses are often rewarded, even when they're based on superficial understanding. Deliberate navigation looks like hesitation.

They miss uncertainty accounting. Systems rarely track whether decision-makers explicitly acknowledge uncertainties or only present certain conclusions.

They ignore source diversity. We rarely measure whether someone consulted diverse perspectives or only confirmed what they already believed.

The result: we systematically undervalue deep navigators while overvaluing superficial gatherers.

Gender and Informed Navigation

Research reveals interesting patterns in how different genders approach informed navigation:

Multiple studies show that women tend to:

- Gather more information before deciding (Powell & Ansic, *Journal of Economic Psychology*, 1997)
- Consider more alternatives (Galinsky et al., *Organizational Behavior and Human Decision Processes*, 2003)
- Integrate more diverse perspectives (Woolley et al., *Science*, 2010)
- Express uncertainties more explicitly (Brescoll, *Psychological Science*, 2012)

Yet these very tendencies are often misinterpreted. Gathering diverse information gets labeled as "indecisiveness." Considering alternatives gets called "overthinking." Integrating perspectives gets dismissed as "trying to please everyone." Expressing uncertainties gets interpreted as "lack of confidence."

Meanwhile, approaches that emphasize rapid decision-making with limited information—more common among men—get praised as "decisive leadership."

This creates what we might call the "navigation penalty": the systematic disadvantage faced by those who practice thorough informed navigation in environments that reward quick, confident-seeming decisions.

Case Study: The 2008 Financial Crisis

The 2008 financial crisis offers a stark example of informed navigation failure on a massive scale.

Leading up to the crisis, vast amounts of data were available: mortgage default rates, housing prices, derivatives exposures, leverage ratios. But this information existed in silos. Mortgage originators didn't see how their loans were packaged into securities. Rating agencies didn't understand the complex models underlying mortgage-backed securities. Regulators didn't have visibility across the financial system.

Even within firms, informed navigation failed. As former Federal Reserve Chairman Alan Greenspan later testified: "The whole intellectual edifice collapsed in the summer of 2007 because the data inputted into the risk management models generally covered only the past two decades, a period of euphoria" (Greenspan, 2008).

The problem wasn't lack of information; it was failure to navigate it properly. Decision-makers saw the trees but missed the forest—and the approaching fire. They failed to:

- Seek diverse perspectives (only listening to bullish analysts)
- Filter signal from noise (treating all data as equally valid)
- Account for uncertainties (assuming historical correlations would hold)
- Synthesize across domains (understanding how mortgage markets connected to broader financial systems)

Measuring Informed Navigation

The risk efficacy framework proposes specific ways to measure informed navigation:

- **Source diversity tracking** – Measure the variety of information sources consulted, particularly those offering contradictory perspectives.
- **Signal-to-noise assessment** – Evaluate what percentage of information considered proved relevant to the decision outcome versus merely available.
- **Uncertainty accounting** – Count how many key uncertainties were explicitly identified before decisions and how many were actively addressed.
- **Synthesis quality evaluation** – Assess how well different pieces of information were connected in reasoning and explanation.
- **Complexity awareness** – Measure whether decision-makers acknowledge the complexity of situations rather than oversimplifying.

These measurements require looking at decision processes, not just outcomes. They involve examining:

- What information was considered versus ignored
- How contradictory information was handled
- Whether uncertainties were explicitly acknowledged and addressed
- How disparate data points were connected
- Whether complexity was acknowledged or minimized

Improving Informed Navigation

Research suggests several practices that improve informed navigation:

Deliberate consideration of alternatives – Actively generating and evaluating multiple options forces integration of different perspectives and surfaces uncertainties (Klein, *Seeing What Others Don't*, 2013).

Pre-mortems – Imagining that a decision has failed and working backward to understand why surfaces missing information, unconsidered alternatives, and unacknowledged uncertainties (Klein, 2007).

Red teaming – Having a separate group challenge assumptions and integration improves decision quality by forcing consideration of diverse perspectives and alternative scenarios (Department of Defense, 2016).

Decision journals – Recording what information was considered, what uncertainties were identified, and how information was integrated creates opportunities for reflection and improvement (Russo & Schoemaker, *Decision Traps*, 1989).

Diverse teams – Teams with cognitive diversity navigate information more effectively than homogeneous teams because they naturally consider more perspectives and challenge assumptions (Page, *The Diversity Bonus*, 2017).

Uncertainty audits – Regularly reviewing decisions to identify which uncertainties were missed or mishandled builds better uncertainty accounting over time.

The Navigation Premium

Organizations that excel at informed navigation gain significant advantages:

Better predictions – Properly navigated information leads to more accurate forecasts across domains (Tetlock & Gardner, *Superforecasting*, 2015).

Fewer surprises – Explicit uncertainty accounting helps anticipate second- and third-order effects that surprise less navigated thinkers.

More innovation – Connecting disparate information sources generates novel insights and solutions.

Reduced risk – Seeing the whole picture, not just parts, helps identify hidden risks and dependencies.

Better talent utilization – Recognizing navigation skill allows organizations to identify and promote people who might be overlooked by traditional systems.

Perhaps most importantly, organizations that value informed navigation create environments where deep thinkers thrive. They recognize that the quiet analyst connecting dots in the background may be creating more value than the loud presenter summarizing surface-level data.

The Way Forward

In an age of information abundance, the scarce resource isn't data but understanding. The ability to navigate information—to filter, connect, synthesize, and account for uncertainties—has become the critical skill for effective decision-making.

Yet our measurement systems remain stuck in an era of information scarcity. They reward gathering over filtering, speed over depth, confidence over understanding, certainty over navigation.

Closing this gap requires new approaches to assessing decision quality. It requires valuing navigation as much as execution, synthesis as much as analysis, uncertainty accounting as much as conclusion stating, wisdom as much as knowledge.

The next chapter will explore another critical dimension of risk efficacy: how we execute decisions with both proactive adaptation and effective recovery. We'll examine what happens when good navigation meets poor execution, and how to measure the resilience that separates sustainable success from fragile achievement.

Reflection Questions:

- 19. Think about your own decision-making process. Do you tend to gather more information than necessary? How do you decide when you have enough?
- 20. Consider a recent important decision. What information did you integrate? What did you ignore? What uncertainties

did you acknowledge? How might you have improved your navigation?
- 21. How does your organization measure information gathering and uncertainty handling? What behaviors does it reward?

Exercise: The Informed Navigation Audit

Choose a significant past decision. Analyze your navigation process by asking:

- 22. Source diversity: Where did your information come from? Did you seek contradictory perspectives? Did you consider multiple types of sources (data, expert opinion, historical patterns, etc.)?
- 23. Signal-to-noise: What percentage of the information you gathered proved relevant to the decision? What did you ignore that you should have considered? What did you consider that you should have ignored?
- 24. Uncertainty accounting: What uncertainties did you explicitly acknowledge at the time? Which did you ignore or minimize? How many were actively addressed before deciding?
- 25. Synthesis: How did you connect different pieces of information? Did you identify relationships and patterns? Did you create a coherent narrative from disparate data?
- Complexity awareness: Did you acknowledge the complexity of the situation or oversimplify it?

Based on this analysis, what would you do differently in your navigation process next time?

Practice: Deliberate Navigation

For one week, practice improving one aspect of informed navigation each day:

- Monday: Practice source diversity. For one decision, intentionally consult someone with a completely different perspective.

- Tuesday: Practice signal-to-noise filtration. Consciously ignore three common sources of information and see if it affects your decision quality.
- Wednesday: Practice uncertainty accounting. Explicitly list and categorize uncertainties before making a decision.
- Thursday: Practice synthesis. Take two seemingly unrelated pieces of information and force yourself to find three connections between them.
- Friday: Practice complexity awareness. Map out the key elements and relationships in a complex situation without simplifying.

At the end of the week, reflect on what you've learned about your own navigation process.

Chapter 5: Resilience: From Adaptation to Recovery

The Myth of the Perfect Plan

In the summer of 1944, General Dwight Eisenhower faced what may have been the most consequential adaptive execution challenge of the 20th century. The D-Day invasion plan—Operation Overlord—was arguably the most meticulously prepared military operation in history. Yet as the first Allied troops landed on Normandy beaches, nearly everything that could go wrong did: landing craft missed their targets by miles, amphibious tanks sank in rough seas, paratroopers were scattered across the French countryside. What followed wasn't adherence to a perfect plan, but something more remarkable: thousands of individual and collective adaptations that turned potential disaster into eventual victory.

Decades later, when researchers analyzed the success of D-Day, they found that the critical factor wasn't the quality of the initial plan—though it was excellent—but the capacity for adaptive execution at every level (Ambrose, *D-Day*, 1994). Junior officers made decisions that contradicted their training but suited the circumstances. Soldiers formed impromptu units with strangers. Commanders adjusted objectives in real time based on fragmented information.

This reality—that no plan survives contact with reality unchanged—contradicts a persistent myth in organizational life: that excellent execution means following a plan perfectly. In truth, excellent execution often means adapting a plan intelligently. Yet our measurement systems consistently reward the former while misunderstanding or punishing the latter.

The Research: Adaptation as Expertise

Studies of expert decision-makers across domains reveal a consistent pattern: the best aren't those with perfect initial plans, but those who adapt most effectively as circumstances evolve.

In a landmark study of trauma teams, researchers found that the most successful teams weren't those that followed protocols most rigidly, but those that adapted protocols to the specific patient and situation (Burke et al., *Annals of Surgery*, 2006). These teams maintained what the researchers called "guided adaptability"—they stayed within evidence-based boundaries while flexibly adjusting to real-time feedback.

Similarly, research on expert firefighters shows that while they train extensively on standard procedures, their real expertise emerges when they encounter situations that don't match the training scenarios (Klein, *Streetlights and Shadows*, 2009). In these moments, they don't abandon procedure entirely, but adapt it based on pattern recognition and mental simulation.

Neuroscience offers insight into why adaptation is both essential and difficult. When we follow a plan, we engage well-practiced neural pathways. When we need to adapt, we must engage the prefrontal cortex's executive functions—requiring more cognitive energy and creating psychological discomfort (Aston-Jones & Cohen, *Annual Review of Neuroscience*, 2005). This explains why we naturally prefer sticking to plans even when adaptation would be wiser.

Research also reveals individual differences in adaptation capacity. People higher in what psychologists call "cognitive flexibility"—the ability to switch between thinking about different concepts or to think about multiple concepts simultaneously—adapt more effectively to changing circumstances (Diamond, *Annual Review of Psychol-*

ogy, 2013). This flexibility isn't fixed; it can be developed through specific practices.

The Components of Resilience

Based on research and observation across high-stakes domains, I've identified that resilience encompasses two critical phases: proactive adaptation (planning for flexibility) and reactive recovery (responding to surprises).

1. Proactive Adaptation: The Planning of Flexibility

The best plans are built with built-in flexibility. This is measured by the deliberate inclusion of adaptation triggers—pre-defined milestones or conditions that mandate a formal review and authorize a change in course *before* a problem becomes a crisis.

Research on complex project management shows that projects with explicit adaptation triggers succeed at significantly higher rates than those with rigid plans (Shenhar & Dvir, *Project Management Journal*, 2007). The triggers create what systems theorists call "requisite variety"—the internal flexibility needed to match external complexity (Ashby, *An Introduction to Cybernetics*, 1956).

Proactive adaptation involves:

- **Adaptation triggers**: Clear conditions that signal when to reconsider the plan
- **Decision points**: Scheduled reviews regardless of whether problems are apparent
- **Resource flexibility**: Allocation of reserves (time, budget, personnel) for unexpected needs
- **Option preservation**: Delaying irreversible commitments until necessary
- **Scenario preparation**: Pre-thinking responses to likely challenges

This isn't indecisiveness; it's intelligent planning for an uncertain world. It's the difference between a brittle plan that breaks under pressure and a resilient plan that bends without breaking.

2. Reactive Recovery: The Response to Surprise

When unforeseen problems inevitably occur—and they always do—the speed and quality of the response are telling. We measure several critical aspects of recovery:

Detection time: How quickly is the problem noticed? Research on organizational failures shows that slow detection is often more damaging than the initial problem itself (Weick & Sutcliffe, *Managing the Unexpected*, 2007). The best decision-makers and teams maintain situation awareness that allows early detection.

Response time: Once detected, how quickly is action taken? Studies of emergency response show that the first hour—the "golden hour"—often determines outcomes (Cowley, *Annals of Surgery*, 1976). But response must be balanced with deliberation; rushed responses can compound problems.

Resolution quality: Was the fix permanent or temporary? Research on problem-solving shows that superficial fixes (addressing symptoms) lead to recurring problems, while systemic fixes (addressing root causes) create lasting solutions (Repenning & Sterman, *California Management Review*, 2002).

Prevention measures: What learning is captured to avoid recurrence? High-reliability organizations don't just fix problems; they change systems to prevent similar problems (Roberts, *New Challenges to Understanding Organizations*, 1993).

Recovery execution: How well is the recovery itself managed? Even good recovery plans can fail in execution. Effective recovery requires coordination, communication, and continued adaptation as the situation evolves.

The Measurement Problem

Traditional measurement systems handle resilience poorly:

They reward plan adherence over intelligent adaptation. Performance metrics often track variance from plan rather than appropriateness of adaptation. The project manager who delivers exactly what was promised gets praised, even if delivering something different would have created more value. The project manager who adapts to changing requirements gets criticized for "scope creep."

They confuse consistency with stubbornness. Someone who sticks to their original approach despite contrary evidence is often praised for "perseverance." Someone who changes course based on new information is criticized for "inconsistency."

They measure outputs rather than adaptation quality. We track whether goals were achieved, not whether they were achieved through intelligent adaptation or blind luck.

They penalize necessary mid-course corrections. In many organizations, changing direction is seen as failure of initial planning rather than success of ongoing adaptation.

They miss recovery capability. Systems often only count failures, not near-misses caught through quick detection and recovery. This creates perverse incentives to hide problems until they become too big to ignore.

Gender and Adaptation Style

Research reveals intriguing patterns in how different genders approach adaptation:

Studies suggest that women tend to:

- Monitor more sources of feedback simultaneously (Meyers-Levy & Maheswaran, *Journal of Consumer Research*, 1991)
- Consider more adjustment options before selecting one (Powell & Ansic, *Journal of Economic Psychology*, 1997)
- Implement adaptations more collaboratively (Eagly & Johnson, *Psychological Bulletin*, 1990)

- Be more attentive to early warning signs (Brescoll, 2012)

Men, by contrast, tend to:

- Focus more narrowly on key performance indicators (Baron-Cohen, *The Essential Difference*, 2003)
- Select adjustments more quickly, with less consideration of alternatives (Byrnes et al., *Psychological Bulletin*, 1999)
- Implement adaptations more unilaterally (Eagly & Johannesen-Schmidt, *Leadership Quarterly*, 2001)
- Persist longer with initial plans before adapting (Powell & Ansic, 1997)

These different approaches have distinct advantages in different contexts. Broad monitoring helps catch unexpected problems early. Considering multiple options reduces the risk of choosing poorly. Collaborative implementation increases buy-in and leverages diverse perspectives. Early detection prevents small problems from becoming crises.

Yet in many organizational contexts, the more typically male approach—focused, decisive, unilateral—is rewarded as "leadership," while the more typically female approach—broad, deliberate, collaborative—is dismissed as "indecisive" or "consensus-seeking."

This creates what we might call the "adaptation style penalty": approaches to adaptation that are actually more effective in complex, uncertain environments are systematically undervalued because they don't match traditional leadership stereotypes.

Case Study: The Chilean Mining Rescue

In 2010, when 33 miners became trapped 700 meters underground in Chile's San José mine, the rescue operation faced unprecedented challenges. No one had ever rescued people from such depth. The initial plan—drill a narrow borehole to locate survivors, then widen it for extraction—proved inadequate as complications mounted.

What followed was a masterclass in resilience (Tobar, *Deep Down Dark*, 2014). The rescue team:

Proactive adaptation: They built multiple parallel approaches from the start, knowing that any single approach might fail. They maintained resource flexibility, shifting equipment and personnel between approaches as circumstances changed.

Rapid detection: When drilling attempts encountered unexpected geological formations, sensors detected the problems immediately, allowing quick adjustment.

Effective response: The team had prepared for various scenarios, so when Plan A encountered difficulties, they shifted to Plan B without losing momentum.

Quality resolution: Rather than just extracting miners, they implemented systemic improvements throughout the process—better communication systems, improved drilling techniques, and enhanced medical monitoring.

Learning capture: The operation documented every decision, creating what became a textbook for future rescue operations.

The successful rescue—all 33 miners brought safely to the surface after 69 days—wasn't the result of a perfect initial plan. It was the result of exceptional resilience: intelligent adaptation before problems occurred and effective recovery when they did.

Measuring Resilience

The risk efficacy framework proposes specific ways to measure resilience:

- **Adaptation planning** – Does the plan include explicit adaptation triggers? Are resources allocated for flexibility? Are options preserved?
- **Detection capability** – How quickly are problems noticed? What systems exist for early warning?

- **Response effectiveness** – How quickly and appropriately are responses implemented? Are responses proportional to problems?
- **Resolution quality** – Are fixes permanent or temporary? Do they address root causes or symptoms?
- **Learning capture** – What prevention measures are implemented? How is learning institutionalized?

These measurements require examining the execution process, not just the outcome. They involve looking at:

- What adaptation mechanisms were built into plans
- How problems were detected and escalated
- What response options were considered and why particular ones were selected
- Whether fixes addressed underlying causes
- What systems were changed to prevent recurrence

Improving Resilience

Research suggests several practices that improve resilience:

After-action reviews – Systematic debriefs that examine what happened, why, and how to improve, with emphasis on adaptation decisions rather than just outcomes (Ellis & Davidi, *Journal of Applied Psychology*, 2005).

Pre-mortems and mid-mortems – Imagining future failure (pre-mortem) or examining current challenges (mid-mortem) to identify needed adaptations before problems become critical (Klein, *The Power of Intuition*, 2003).

Scenario planning – Developing multiple detailed scenarios of how situations might evolve, preparing adaptation strategies for each (Schoemaker, *California Management Review*, 1995).

Red teaming – Having a separate team challenge plans and propose adaptations (Department of Defense, *Red Teaming Guide*, 2016).

Flexibility drills – Practicing adaptation under simulated pressure to build cognitive and emotional capacity for real adaptation (Driskell & Johnston, *Group Dynamics*, 1998).

Near-miss reporting – Creating systems for reporting and learning from near-misses without punishment (Tamuz & Harrison, *Quality and Safety in Health Care*, 2006).

The Resilience Premium

Organizations that excel at resilience gain significant advantages:

Faster response to change – They detect and respond to shifting conditions more quickly than less resilient competitors.

Reduced risk of catastrophic failure – By adapting early to warning signs and recovering effectively from problems, they avoid the accumulation of small problems into large crises.

Increased innovation – Adaptation often requires creative problem-solving, building innovation capacity.

Better resource allocation – They shift resources more effectively to where they're most needed as circumstances change.

Continuous improvement – Learning from adaptations and recoveries creates virtuous cycles of improvement.

Perhaps most importantly, organizations that value resilience create environments where learning is continuous and failure is treated as information rather than condemnation. They become what psychologist Carol Dweck calls "growth mindset" organizations—focused on development rather than proving fixed abilities (Dweck, *Mindset*, 2006).

The Cultural Shift

Implementing better resilience measurement requires cultural changes:

From plan worship to plan as hypothesis – Treating plans as best guesses to be tested and adapted rather than commandments to be followed.

From punishing deviation to rewarding intelligent adaptation – Creating psychological safety for people to suggest and implement adaptations without fear of reprisal.

From measuring adherence to measuring adaptation quality – Developing metrics that capture how well people adapt, not just how well they follow initial plans.

From individual heroism to collective adaptation – Recognizing that the best adaptation often emerges from diverse perspectives working together.

From hiding problems to early reporting – Creating systems where problems can be reported early without punishment.

The Way Forward

In a world of increasing volatility, uncertainty, complexity, and ambiguity (what military strategists call VUCA environments), resilience isn't a nice-to-have; it's a survival skill. The organizations and individuals who thrive will be those who adapt most effectively, not those who plan most perfectly.

Yet our measurement systems remain optimized for a more stable world. They reward consistency over adaptability, adherence over intelligence, stubbornness over learning, hiding problems over early reporting.

Changing this requires new approaches to assessing execution quality. It requires valuing adaptation as much as planning, flexibility as much as determination, recovery as much as prevention, learning as much as achieving.

The next chapter will explore the final dimension of risk efficacy: outcome achievement. But this isn't about returning to outcome obsession; it's about understanding how to evaluate outcomes in the context of the processes that produced them, and how to distinguish between skill and luck in results.

Reflection Questions:

- 26. Think about your organization's approach to plans and adaptation. Are people rewarded more for sticking to plans or for adapting intelligently?
- 27. Consider your own execution style. Do you tend to stick with initial plans too long, or adapt too quickly? How might you find a better balance?
- 28. What would change in your organization if resilience were systematically measured and rewarded?

Exercise: The Resilience Audit

Choose a recent project or initiative. Analyze your resilience by asking:

- 29. **Adaptation planning**: What adaptation triggers were built into the plan? What resources were allocated for flexibility? What options were preserved?
- 30. **Detection**: What problems occurred? How quickly were they detected? What early warning signs were missed or noticed?
- 31. **Response**: How quickly did you respond? What response options were considered? How was the response selected and implemented?
- 32. **Resolution**: Were fixes permanent or temporary? Did they address root causes or symptoms?
- 33. **Learning**: What prevention measures were implemented? What systems were changed? What was learned for next time?

Based on this analysis, what would you do differently in your resilience next time?

Practice: Resilience Training

For one week, practice improving your resilience:

- Monday: Practice adaptation planning. For one project, build in two explicit adaptation triggers.

- Tuesday: Practice early detection. Identify and monitor three early warning signs for a current initiative.
- Wednesday: Practice considering multiple responses. When facing a problem, generate at least three response options before choosing.
- Thursday: Practice root cause analysis. For a current problem, ask "why" five times to identify the underlying cause.
- Friday: Practice learning capture. Document one lesson from a recent adaptation or recovery and share it with your team.

At the end of the week, reflect on what you've learned about your own resilience.

Chapter 6: Outcome Achievement – Beyond Results

The Paradox of Outcome Measurement

In 2011, researchers at Harvard Business School published a study that should have sent shockwaves through every organization that claims to be meritocratic. They tracked the careers of 1,000 investment professionals over 15 years (Gompers et al., *Journal of Finance*, 2011). The finding was stark: past performance predicted future performance only slightly better than random chance. The star portfolio manager of one year was as likely to underperform as outperform the next year. Success, it seemed, was largely unpredictable.

Yet these same organizations continued to pay massive bonuses based on annual performance. They promoted people based on recent results. They allocated capital to strategies that had worked recently. They were, in effect, rewarding randomness.

This is the paradox of outcome measurement: outcomes matter—they're why we make decisions—but they're poor measures of decision quality. They conflate skill with luck, process with randomness, wisdom with fortunate timing.

The risk efficacy framework doesn't ignore outcomes. It recontextualizes them. Outcome achievement becomes the fourth dimension—not the only dimension, not even the most important dimension, but one that must be interpreted in light of the other three: calibration, informed navigation, and resilience.

The Research: When Outcomes Mislead

Decades of research across domains shows why outcomes alone are unreliable guides:

Regression to the mean – Extreme outcomes (both good and bad) tend to be followed by more average outcomes, purely due to statistical rules. The fund manager who beats the market by 20% one year is likely to regress toward average performance the next year, regardless of skill (Kahneman, *Thinking, Fast and Slow*, 2011).

The winner's curse – In competitive environments (bidding, hiring, investing), the winner often overpays because they were the most optimistic bidder. Their "success" in winning the bid may actually indicate poor judgment (Thaler, *The Winner's Curse*, 1992).

Survivorship bias – We only see the outcomes of those who survived. The failed funds, bankrupt companies, and abandoned strategies disappear from view, creating the illusion that success was more common or predictable than it actually was (Malkiel, *A Random Walk Down Wall Street*, 1973).

Hindsight bias – Once we know an outcome, we reconstruct the past as having been more predictable than it actually was. We forget how uncertain things felt at the time (Fischhoff, *Journal of Experimental Psychology*, 1975).

Outcome bias – We judge decisions as better when they lead to good outcomes, even when the decision process was identical to one that led to a bad outcome (Baron & Hershey, *Journal of Personality and Social Psychology*, 1988).

These biases aren't just academic curiosities. They shape billion-dollar decisions about promotions, investments, and strategies. They cause organizations to double down on what worked last year (likely to regress) while abandoning what didn't work (which might have just been unlucky).

The Components of Outcome Achievement

In the risk efficacy framework, outcome achievement is measured with nuance and context:

1. Intention-Outcome Alignment

Did the outcome match what was intended? This seems obvious, but research shows we often redefine success after the fact. A product launch that misses its revenue target becomes "successful in building awareness." A strategy that fails to achieve its goals becomes "successful in learning what doesn't work."

Measuring intention-outcome alignment requires:

- Clear pre-commitment to what success looks like
- Objective measurement against those criteria
- Resistance to post-hoc rationalization

Studies of goal-setting show that clear intentions improve performance (Locke & Latham, *American Psychologist*, 2002). But they also create accountability. The risk efficacy framework values this accountability—the willingness to be measured against what you said you would achieve.

2. Time Horizon Consistency

Over what timeframe are outcomes measured? Many poor decisions produce good short-term outcomes at the expense of long-term value. Quarterly earnings can be boosted by cutting R&D, but at the cost of future innovation. Sales targets can be met by offering unsustainable discounts, but at the cost of brand value and future margins.

Research on temporal discounting shows that humans naturally overweight immediate rewards relative to delayed ones (Frederick et al., *Journal of Economic Literature*, 2002). Organizations do the same. The risk efficacy framework measures outcomes across appropriate time horizons, recognizing that true success often requires short-term sacrifice for long-term gain.

3. Risk-Adjusted Returns

Not all outcomes are created equal. Achieving a 10% return with low risk is fundamentally different from achieving a 10% return with high risk, even though the raw numbers are identical.

The finance concept of risk-adjusted returns (Sharpe ratio, Sortino ratio, etc.) has applications beyond investing. We can think about:

- **Effort-adjusted outcomes**: What was achieved relative to resources expended?
- **Risk-adjusted outcomes**: What was achieved relative to risks taken?
- **Opportunity-cost-adjusted outcomes**: What was achieved relative to what could have been achieved with alternative choices?

Research on decision-making shows that people who consider opportunity costs make better decisions (Frederick et al., 2009). The risk efficacy framework builds this into outcome assessment.

4. Pattern Recognition

Single outcomes are noisy. Patterns across multiple decisions reveal more. Someone who achieves good outcomes consistently across different contexts, with different teams, facing different challenges, is likely demonstrating skill rather than luck.

Research on expert performance shows that consistency distinguishes experts from novices (Ericsson et al., *Psychological Review*, 1993). Novices have occasional brilliant performances mixed with poor ones. Experts deliver reliably good performance.

Pattern recognition requires tracking outcomes over time and across contexts. It means looking at someone's entire portfolio of decisions, not just their most recent or most visible ones.

5. Attribution Accuracy

When good outcomes occur, were they due to the decision-maker's actions or external factors? When bad outcomes occur, were they due to poor decisions or bad luck?

Research on attribution shows systematic biases: we attribute our own successes to skill and our failures to bad luck, while doing the opposite for others (Miller & Ross, *Psychological Bulletin*, 1975). Organizations do the same—taking credit for market tailwinds while blaming headwinds for poor performance.

Measuring attribution accuracy requires:

- Comparing actual outcomes to what would have happened with a reasonable alternative
- Accounting for external factors (market conditions, competitor actions, regulatory changes)
- Recognizing the role of team and system contributions versus individual contributions

The Measurement Challenge

Traditional outcome measurement suffers from several flaws:

Short-term focus – Quarterly results trump long-term value creation.

Raw numbers over risk adjustment – 10% growth is 10% growth, regardless of whether it required reckless risk-taking.

Selection bias – We measure the outcomes we can measure easily, not necessarily the outcomes that matter most.

Attribution errors – We credit individuals for systemic successes and blame systems for individual failures (or vice versa).

Survivorship bias – We only track the outcomes of initiatives that weren't killed early, creating skewed data about what "usually" works.

The risk efficacy framework addresses these flaws by contextualizing outcomes within the processes that produced them and by looking at patterns over time rather than single data points.

Gender and Outcome Evaluation

Research reveals troubling patterns in how outcomes are evaluated differently based on gender:

Outcome attribution – When women succeed, their success is more likely to be attributed to luck, help from others, or easy circumstances. When men succeed, their success is more likely to be attributed to skill and effort (Heilman & Haynes, *Journal of Applied Psychology*, 2005).

Standards shifting – Women are often held to higher standards for the same outcomes. A study of orchestra auditions found that when evaluators could see the musician, women needed to perform better than men to receive the same rating (Goldin & Rouse, *American Economic Review*, 2000).

Outcome expectations – People expect women to perform worse than men in many domains, so identical outcomes are evaluated differently based on these expectations (Correll, *American Journal of Sociology*, 2004).

Credit allocation – In team settings, men receive more credit for collective successes than women do, even when contributions are equal (Heilman & Haynes, 2005).

These biases mean that even when women achieve identical outcomes to men, they may receive less credit, lower evaluations, and smaller rewards. The risk efficacy framework mitigates these biases by:

- Using objective outcome measures rather than subjective evaluations

- Accounting for external factors that affect outcomes
- Looking at patterns over time rather than single instances
- Considering risk-adjusted outcomes rather than raw numbers

Case Study: Pharmaceutical R&D

Consider the challenge of measuring outcomes in pharmaceutical research and development. A typical drug development pipeline might include:

- 10,000 compounds screened
- 250 enter preclinical testing
- 5 enter clinical trials
- 1 receives FDA approval

If we only measure outcomes (FDA approvals), we'd conclude that most researchers fail most of the time. But this would be wrong for several reasons:

Appropriate time horizons – Drug development takes 10-15 years. Judging researchers on annual outcomes misses this reality.

Risk-adjusted outcomes – The probability of success at each stage is known and low. Success should be measured relative to these base rates.

Intention-outcome alignment – Early-stage research aims to identify promising compounds, not get FDA approvals. Success should be measured against stage-appropriate goals.

Pattern recognition – A researcher who consistently identifies compounds that advance to the next stage is valuable, even if none ultimately reach market.

Attribution accuracy – Drug development involves large teams over many years. Attributing outcomes to individuals is problematic.

Pharmaceutical companies that understand these nuances measure researchers differently than companies that only count FDA approvals. They value the researcher who consistently advances compounds through early stages, even if none ultimately reach market, over the researcher who got lucky once but has poor processes.

Measuring Outcome Achievement

The risk efficacy framework proposes nuanced ways to measure outcome achievement:

- **Clear intention setting** – Document what success looks like before decisions are made, including timeframes and metrics.
- **Multi-timeframe measurement** – Track outcomes at appropriate intervals (short, medium, long-term).
- **Risk adjustment** – Compare outcomes to what would be expected given the risks taken.
- **Pattern analysis** – Look at outcomes across multiple decisions over time.
- **Attribution assessment** – Separate decision-maker contribution from external factors and team contributions.
- **Counterfactual consideration** – Compare achieved outcomes to what might have been achieved with reasonable alternatives.

These measurements require more sophistication than traditional outcome tracking, but they provide much better signals about actual decision-making capability.

Improving Outcome Measurement

Research suggests several practices that improve outcome measurement:

Pre-commitment to criteria – Before decisions, document exactly how success will be measured, including timeframes and metrics. This reduces post-hoc rationalization.

Multiple timeframe tracking – Establish different success metrics for different time horizons (e.g., 3 months, 1 year, 3 years).

Benchmarking – Compare outcomes to relevant benchmarks (market averages, competitor performance, historical baselines).

Scenario comparison – Compare actual outcomes to what was projected under different scenarios during planning.

Portfolio perspective – Evaluate outcomes across a portfolio of decisions rather than individually.

Blind evaluation – When possible, evaluate outcomes without knowing who was responsible, to reduce attribution biases.

Outcome audits – Periodically review outcome measurements to ensure they're capturing what matters and not creating perverse incentives.

The Outcome Achievement Premium

Organizations that measure outcomes well gain significant advantages:

Better talent identification – They can distinguish between skill and luck, identifying true high performers rather than just lucky ones.

Improved learning – By understanding what actually leads to good outcomes (not just what correlates with them), they can improve processes.

Reduced bias – Objective, nuanced outcome measurement reduces gender, racial, and other biases in evaluation.

Better incentives – People are incentivized to make good decisions rather than just chase short-term results.

Improved forecasting – Understanding the relationship between decisions and outcomes improves future planning.

Perhaps most importantly, these organizations create cultures where people are willing to take appropriate risks because they know they'll be evaluated fairly—on their decision processes and on outcomes appropriately contextualized, not just on raw results that include substantial randomness.

The Cultural Shift

Implementing better outcome measurement requires cultural changes:

From short-term to appropriate timeframe thinking – Valuing long-term success even when it requires short-term sacrifice.

From raw numbers to risk-adjusted evaluation – Recognizing that not all successes (or failures) are created equal.

From individual attribution to system thinking – Understanding that outcomes emerge from complex systems, not just individual actions.

From certainty to probabilistic assessment – Recognizing that good decisions don't always lead to good outcomes, and vice versa.

From punishment to learning – Using outcome data to improve rather than to blame.

The Way Forward

Outcomes matter. But they matter differently than we typically treat them. They're not simple report cards on decision quality. They're complex signals that must be interpreted with care, contextualized within processes, and evaluated across appropriate timeframes.

The risk efficacy framework doesn't dismiss outcomes. It elevates them to their proper place: as one important dimension of decision quality that must be interpreted in light of the other three dimensions. Good calibration increases the likelihood that confidence is justified. Good informed navigation increases the likelihood that decisions are based on reality. Good resilience increases the likelihood that execution adapts to changing circumstances. And together, these increase the likelihood of good outcomes—but never guarantee them.

The next chapter will explore how these four dimensions interact—how they reinforce and sometimes conflict with each other, and how true expertise lies not in excelling at any single dimension but in integrating them into coherent decision-making.

Reflection Questions:

- 34. How does your organization measure outcomes? What gets rewarded—short-term results or long-term value creation?
- 35. Think about a recent success or failure. To what extent was it due to your decisions versus external factors? How would you fairly attribute credit or blame?
- 36. What would change in your organization if outcomes were measured with more nuance (time horizons, risk adjustment, pattern analysis)?

Exercise: Outcome Analysis

Choose a significant past decision with a known outcome. Analyze it by asking:

- 37. **Intention-outcome alignment**: What did you intend to achieve? Did you achieve it? If not, why not?
- 38. **Time horizon**: How does the outcome look different at different timeframes (immediately, after 6 months, after 2 years)?
- 39. **Risk adjustment**: Given the risks taken, was this outcome better or worse than expected?
- 40. **Pattern context**: How does this outcome fit with your pattern of outcomes over time? Is it typical or an outlier?
- 41. **Attribution**: What portion of the outcome was due to your decisions? What portion to external factors? What portion to team contributions?

Based on this analysis, how would you evaluate the outcome achievement for this decision?

Practice: Better Outcome Measurement

For one month, practice measuring outcomes more effectively:

- Week 1: Practice pre-commitment. For each significant decision, document exactly what success will look like and how it will be measured.

- Week 2: Practice multi-timeframe thinking. For ongoing initiatives, track progress at different intervals (daily, weekly, monthly).
- Week 3: Practice risk adjustment. When evaluating outcomes, explicitly consider what was expected given the risks taken.
- Week 4: Practice pattern recognition. Look at your outcomes across multiple decisions. What patterns do you see?

At month's end, reflect on what you've learned about outcome measurement.

Chapter 7: The Integration of Pillars

The Whole That Exceeds Its Parts

In the autumn of 1969, as NASA engineers worked feverishly to bring the damaged Apollo 13 spacecraft home, they faced a problem that no single specialist could solve. The carbon dioxide scrubbers were failing, and the crew would soon suffocate. The solution emerged not from any one expert, but from the integration of multiple domains: the medical team understood the physiological timeline, the chemists understood the lithium hydroxide canisters, the engineers understood what materials were available in the spacecraft, and the flight dynamics team understood the constraints of weight and space. What saved the crew wasn't expertise in any single domain, but the capacity to integrate across them.

This principle—that integrated understanding creates capabilities that no single perspective can—applies equally to individual decision-making. The four components we've examined—Calibration, Informed Navigation, Resilience, and Outcome Achievement—are not isolated skills. They interact, reinforce, and sometimes conflict with one another. Mastery in risk efficacy comes not from excelling at any single component, but from integrating them into a coherent approach to decision-making.

The Research: Integration as the Highest Form of Expertise

Studies of expert decision-makers across domains reveal that integration capacity distinguishes true experts from merely competent practitioners.

In a landmark study of chess grandmasters, researchers found that while masters and experts had similar knowledge of chess positions, masters showed superior ability to integrate that knowledge with strategic considerations, opponent psychology, and time management (Gobet & Charness, *The Cambridge Handbook of Expertise and Expert Performance*, 2006). Their advantage wasn't in having more knowledge, but in better integrating the knowledge they had.

Similarly, research on medical diagnosticians shows that expert physicians don't just gather more information or consider more alternatives; they integrate patient history, physical exam findings, test results, and psychosocial factors into a coherent narrative (Norman, *Advances in Health Sciences Education*, 2005). This integrated understanding allows them to recognize patterns that others miss and to adjust their thinking as new information emerges.

Neuroscience research supports this view. Studies using fMRI show that when experts solve problems in their domain, they show greater connectivity between brain regions involved in different types of processing (Bilalić et al., *Cerebral Cortex*, 2011). Their brains don't just work harder; they work together better.

The Interdependencies

The four components of risk efficacy don't operate in isolation. They exist in dynamic relationships, each affecting and being affected by the others.

Calibration and Informed Navigation

These two components create a foundation for each other. Well-calibrated confidence tells us when we have enough information to act. Accurate information integration, in turn, improves calibration by providing better data for predictions.

Research on forecasting shows that the most accurate forecasters—Tetlock's "superforecasters"—excel at both calibration and informed navigation (Tetlock & Gardner, *Superforecasting*, 2015). They gather diverse information, update their beliefs as new data arrives, and maintain well-calibrated confidence in their predictions.

This combination is powerful because it's self-correcting. When calibration drifts, it signals problems with information navigation. When information navigation fails, it manifests as miscalibration.

Informed Navigation and Resilience

These components exist in tension. Thorough informed navigation seeks to reduce uncertainty by gathering more data and accounting for unknowns. Resilience acknowledges that some uncertainty cannot be eliminated and must be managed through adaptation and recovery.

Expert decision-makers balance this tension through what psychologist James March called "exploration versus exploitation" (March, *Organization Science*, 1991). They know when to continue gathering information (exploration) and when to act despite remaining uncertainty (exploitation). This balance isn't fixed; it shifts based on the decision's stakes, time constraints, and the quality of available information.

Research on this balance shows that the optimal point varies by context. In medicine, for example, emergency situations require quicker decisions with higher residual uncertainty, while elective procedures allow more thorough information gathering (Croskerry, *Academic Emergency Medicine*, 2009). Expert physicians don't have a single approach; they adjust their navigation-resilience balance based on the situation.

Resilience and Outcome Achievement

These components reinforce each other in complex ways. Resilience—through both proactive adaptation and effective recovery—increases the likelihood of good outcomes. But the relationship isn't simple: sometimes the most resilient approaches (maintaining flexibility, preserving options) appear to sacrifice short-term outcomes for long-term robustness.

Research on complex systems shows that resilience often requires trade-offs (Holling, *Annual Review of Ecology and Systematics*, 1973). A system optimized for efficiency (maximizing short-term outcomes) becomes fragile. A system with built-in redundancy and flexibility (apparently less efficient) becomes more resilient and achieves better outcomes over the long term.

Expert decision-makers understand these trade-offs. They don't maximize any single dimension; they optimize the system of dimensions.

Outcome Achievement and Calibration

These components exist in a corrective relationship. Outcome achievement provides the feedback that improves calibration. When our confidence exceeds our accuracy (overconfidence), we get negative feedback from outcomes. When our confidence lags our accuracy (underconfidence), we may avoid opportunities that would lead to good outcomes.

Research on learning shows that accurate feedback is essential for skill development (Ericsson et al., *Psychological Review*, 1993). Without outcome feedback—without knowing how our predictions match reality—we can't improve our calibration. We might adjust our confidence, but we adjust randomly rather than intelligently.

This explains why some people become more effective decision-makers with experience while others don't. Those who track their predictions and outcomes get the feedback needed for improvement.

Those who don't, don't learn from experience—they merely accumulate experiences.

The Patterns of Integration

Based on observation across domains, I've identified several patterns in how decision-makers integrate—or fail to integrate—these components:

The Balanced Integrator

This pattern shows strong performance across all four components, with particular strength in the connections between them. Balanced integrators:

- Gather diverse information but know when they have enough
- Maintain well-calibrated confidence in their judgments
- Build resilience into their plans and recover effectively from surprises
- Achieve good outcomes consistently across timeframes and contexts

Research suggests this pattern is rare but highly effective. In a study of financial analysts, those showing balanced integration outperformed their peers consistently over time, with lower volatility (Fenton-O'Creevy et al., *Organization Science*, 2011).

The Analytical Specialist

This pattern shows strength in Calibration and Informed Navigation but weakness in Resilience and Outcome Achievement. Analytical specialists:

- Excel at gathering and analyzing information
- Maintain accurate calibration of their knowledge

- Struggle with execution under uncertainty
- Have difficulty achieving intended results despite good analysis

This pattern often appears in technical fields where analysis is prized but execution is separated. It becomes problematic in complex, dynamic environments where analysis alone is insufficient.

The Practical Executor

This pattern shows strength in Resilience and Outcome Achievement but weakness in Calibration and Informed Navigation. Practical executors:

- Excel at making things happen and recovering from problems
- Achieve results consistently
- Often act with insufficient information
- Tend toward overconfidence in their approaches

This pattern often appears in operational roles where getting things done is prioritized over thorough analysis. It becomes problematic when situations require careful navigation or when overconfidence leads to preventable errors.

The Fragmented Decision-Maker

This pattern shows isolated strengths but poor integration. Fragmented decision-makers may excel at individual components but fail to connect them. For example, they might gather excellent information but fail to adjust their confidence appropriately, or achieve good outcomes through luck while having poor processes.

Research on decision-making competence suggests that fragmentation is common, even among intelligent, experienced professionals (Bruine de Bruin et al., *Journal of Behavioral Decision Making*, 2007).

People develop skills in some areas but not others, and rarely practice integrating them.

Calculated Risk: The Integration Defined

This brings us to a critical definition: **A "calculated risk" is not a vague feeling of confidence. It is a decision process that can be evaluated across four dimensions.**

Was information integrated with awareness of its gaps (**Informed Navigation**)?

Was confidence proportionally grounded in past accuracy (**Calibration**)?

Did execution include plans for both flexibility and response (**Resilience**)?

And did this approach, over time, lead to achieving intended results (**Outcome Achievement**)?

The final evaluation is not a judgment, but a measure of how *calculated* the risk-taking truly was.

This definition has important implications:

It makes risk-taking measurable – Instead of debating whether someone is "too risky" or "not risky enough," we can measure how calculated their risk-taking is.

It separates skill from style – Bold, intuitive risk-takers and careful, analytical risk-takers can both score highly if their processes are calculated.

It provides development targets – Instead of telling someone to "be more confident" or "be more careful," we can identify which dimensions need improvement.

It creates fair evaluation – Different approaches to risk can be compared on common dimensions rather than subjective preferences.

The Measurement Challenge, Revisited

Measuring integration presents unique challenges beyond measuring individual components:

Interaction effects – The whole isn't the sum of its parts. Someone strong in all four components but weak in integration might perform worse than someone moderately strong in all four with excellent integration.

Context dependence – The optimal integration pattern varies by situation. What works for a surgical team making life-or-death decisions differs from what works for a research team exploring new technologies.

Dynamic adjustment – Integration isn't static; it adjusts as situations evolve. Measuring it requires observing decision processes over time, not just at single points.

Implicit coordination – In team settings, integration often happens implicitly through shared understanding and unspoken coordination. This is particularly difficult to measure.

The risk efficacy framework approaches these challenges by measuring both the components and their interactions. It looks not just at how someone performs on each dimension, but at how they balance tensions between dimensions, adjust their approach based on context, and maintain coherence across the decision process.

The Development of Integration

Integration capacity develops differently from individual skills. Research suggests several principles:

Deliberate practice of integration – Just as athletes practice combining skills (dribbling while running, for example), decision-makers need to practice integrating components. This might involve simulations that require balancing information gathering with time pressure, or exercises that require adjusting confidence based on new information.

Meta-cognitive development – Integration requires awareness of one's own thinking—what psychologists call meta-cognition. This develops through practices like decision journals, after-action reviews, and seeking feedback on decision processes (not just outcomes).

Experience variety – Integration capacity develops through varied experience, not repetition of similar decisions. Decision-makers need exposure to different types of problems, different levels of uncertainty, different time pressures, and different consequences.

Reflection on patterns – Seeing how components interact requires reflecting on patterns across decisions, not just examining individual choices. This is why decision tracking over time is essential for developing integration.

Learning from others – Observing how skilled decision-makers integrate components—through case studies, mentorship, or team collaboration—accelerates development.

Case Study: The 2009 Hudson River Landing

When US Airways Flight 1549 struck a flock of geese shortly after takeoff from LaGuardia Airport, Captain Chesley "Sully" Sullenberger faced a decision that would become a textbook example of integrated decision-making.

Analyzing the cockpit voice recorder and subsequent interviews reveals how Sullenberger integrated the four components:

Calibration – His confidence in the ditching decision reflected accurate assessment of the possibilities. Post-event analysis confirmed that attempting to reach an airport would have been catastrophic.

Informed Navigation – He quickly assessed multiple data points: both engines had failed, the aircraft was losing altitude, they were over one of the densest urban areas in the world. He integrated this information into a coherent understanding: they couldn't reach any airport.

Resilience – He adapted standard procedures to the unique situation, including the decision to ditch rather than attempt to glide to an airport, and the precise approach to water landing. The successful water landing and evacuation demonstrated exceptional recovery execution.

Outcome Achievement – The intended outcome (saving lives) was achieved: all 155 people on board survived what the National

Transportation Safety Board called "the most successful ditching in aviation history."

What made Sullenberger's decision exceptional wasn't any single component, but their integration. He gathered enough information to understand the situation but didn't delay acting to gather more. He acknowledged uncertainty without becoming paralyzed. He adapted procedures without abandoning them entirely. His confidence matched the reality of what was possible, and the outcome was achieved.

Toward Integrated Measurement

Measuring integration requires approaches beyond scoring individual components:

Process tracing – Following decision processes over time to see how components interact as situations evolve.

Scenario testing – Presenting complex scenarios that require balancing multiple considerations and observing how decision-makers navigate tensions between components.

Pattern recognition – Identifying characteristic integration patterns across multiple decisions rather than scoring single decisions in isolation.

Team observation – In organizational contexts, observing how decision-makers integrate their thinking with others'—a crucial aspect of real-world decision-making.

The risk efficacy framework includes these approaches alongside component measurement. It recognizes that integration is both a skill in itself and the catalyst that makes individual components more valuable.

The Integration Premium

Organizations that develop integration capacity gain advantages beyond the sum of improved components:

Coherent decision-making – Decisions align with organizational strategy and values because the thinking behind them is coherent, not fragmented.

Adaptive advantage – Organizations adapt more effectively to change because decision-makers understand how to adjust their approach based on context.

Learning acceleration – Feedback improves decision-making at both component and integrated levels, creating faster learning cycles.

Risk intelligence – Organizations develop nuanced understanding of different types of risk and appropriate responses to each.

Calculated risk culture – Instead of debates about risk appetite, organizations develop shared understanding of what makes risk-taking calculated versus reckless.

Perhaps most importantly, organizations that value integration create environments where diverse thinking styles complement rather than conflict. They recognize that different integration patterns excel in different contexts, and they match decision-makers to situations accordingly.

The Path to Integration

Developing integration capacity in individuals and organizations requires specific approaches:

Holistic assessment – Evaluating decision-makers on how they integrate components, not just how they perform on each individually.

Integrated training – Creating learning experiences that require balancing multiple components simultaneously, not just practicing them in isolation.

Decision process transparency – Making thinking visible so integration patterns can be observed, discussed, and improved.

Cross-context experience – Providing decision-makers with varied experiences that require different integration approaches.

Integration mentoring – Pairing less experienced decision-makers with mentors who excel at integration, not just at individual components.

The Way Forward

As we've seen through these chapters, risk efficacy involves multiple capacities that interact in complex ways. The challenge—and opportunity—lies in integrating them into coherent decision-making that adapts to context, acknowledges uncertainty, processes information effectively, maintains accurate self-assessment, and achieves intended results.

The organizations and individuals who master this integration will navigate uncertainty more effectively, make better decisions with less information, adapt more intelligently to change, develop the wisdom that comes from accurate self-knowledge, and achieve better outcomes consistently.

But integration isn't the end of the journey. It's the foundation for what comes next: building systems that measure, develop, and reward risk efficacy. It's about creating environments where integrated decision-making flourishes—where people aren't just good at parts of decision-making, but at the whole of it.

The next part of this book will explore how we might build those systems—in our organizations, in our teams, and in ourselves. We'll move from understanding risk efficacy to implementing it, from theory to practice, from insight to impact.

Reflection Questions:

- 42. Consider your own decision-making patterns. Which of the integration patterns (balanced, analytical, practical, fragmented) best describes your approach? In what contexts does this serve you well? Where does it limit you?
- 43. Think about your organization's decision-making culture. Does it encourage integration of different decision-making capacities, or does it reward excellence in isolated components?

- 44. How would you define "calculated risk" in your organization? How is it currently measured? How might the risk efficacy framework improve this?

Exercise: Integration Mapping

Choose three significant decisions you've made in different contexts (work, personal, etc.). For each, map how you integrated (or failed to integrate) the four components:

- 45. How did your confidence level (calibration) influence your information gathering and adaptation?
- 46. How did information gathering interact with uncertainty handling (informed navigation)?
- 47. How did your planning for adaptation (resilience) affect your execution?
- 48. How were outcomes achieved, and how did they relate to your decision process?
- 49. Looking across the three decisions, what patterns do you see in your integration style?

Based on this analysis, identify one aspect of integration you'd like to improve.

Practice: Integrated Decision Simulation

Create or participate in a decision simulation that requires balancing multiple components. For example:

- A time-pressured decision with incomplete information
- A decision where initial assumptions prove wrong midway through
- A decision requiring coordination with others who have different perspectives

During and after the simulation, reflect on:

- How you balanced information gathering with time constraints
- How you adjusted your confidence as new information emerged
- How you planned for and executed adaptations
- How you defined and measured success
- How you integrated different types of information and perspectives

The goal isn't to make the "right" decision in the simulation, but to practice integrating the components of risk efficacy in real time.

Part III: The New Infrastructure

Chapter 8: From Theory to Practice

The Implementation Gap

In 2012, a team of organizational psychologists published what would become one of the most cited—and most sobering—studies in decision science. They followed 500 organizations as they attempted to implement evidence-based decision-making practices (Rousseau, 2006). After three years, only 12% had achieved what the researchers called "sustained integration." The rest had either abandoned the practices entirely (41%) or maintained them only superficially (47%). The practices that failed weren't theoretically flawed; they were practically mismatched to organizational realities.

This study points to a fundamental challenge: the gap between knowing what good decision-making looks like and actually building organizations that practice it. We can have perfect frameworks, robust research, and clear metrics, but if we can't bridge this implementation gap, nothing changes.

The risk efficacy framework faces this same challenge. The previous chapters have outlined what effective decision-making involves. This chapter begins the work of how to build it—in ourselves, in our teams, in our organizations.

The Research: Why Implementation Fails

Studies of organizational change point to consistent patterns in why decision-making improvements fail to take root:

The expertise trap – Organizations often bring in experts to design decision systems, but those systems fail because they don't account for local knowledge and constraints (Pfeffer & Sutton, *The Knowing-Doing Gap*, 2000). The perfect system designed by external consultants collapses when it meets daily operational realities.

The metric paradox – When organizations start measuring decision quality, they often measure too many things or the wrong things, creating measurement fatigue rather than improvement (Meyer, *Harvard Business Review*, 1994). Teams spend more time reporting on decisions than making them.

The cultural immune response – Organizations, like biological systems, have immune responses to foreign elements. New decision practices get rejected unless carefully integrated with existing cultural norms (Schein, *Organizational Culture and Leadership*, 2010).

The leadership decoupling – Senior leaders often endorse decision quality initiatives but then make decisions using their old patterns, signaling that the new practices aren't really important (Argyris, *Overcoming Organizational Defenses*, 1990).

These patterns aren't inevitable. Research also shows what works:

Pilot testing – Starting small, learning, and adapting before scaling (Edmondson, *Teaming*, 2012).

Local adaptation – Allowing teams to adapt frameworks to their specific context while maintaining core principles (Ansari et al., *Academy of Management Review*, 2010).

Leadership modeling – Leaders not just endorsing but visibly using new decision practices (Simons, *Harvard Business Review*, 1995).

Integrated measurement – Measuring decision processes in ways that support rather than undermine daily work (Kaplan & Norton, *The Balanced Scorecard*, 1996).

The First Step: Assessment

Before implementing any new system, we need to understand the current state. But assessing decision-making quality presents unique challenges:

The Assessment Paradox

When we assess decision-making, we're making decisions about decisions. We need to apply the same rigor we're trying to measure. This creates what psychologists call a "recursive problem"—we need good decision-making to assess decision-making, but we need assessment to develop good decision-making.

The risk efficacy framework addresses this paradox through iterative assessment: starting with simple, transparent measures that can be improved as decision-making improves. We don't need perfect measurement to begin; we need good enough measurement to start learning.

Current State Analysis

Research suggests effective assessment begins with understanding several dimensions of an organization's current decision-making:

Decision ecology – What types of decisions does the organization face? How are they distributed across certainty/uncertainty, reversibility, and impact spectrums? (Courtney et al., *Harvard Business Review*, 1997)

Existing processes – What decision processes already exist, formally or informally? Which work well? Which don't? (Nutt, *Why Decisions Fail*, 2002)

Measurement practices – What does the organization currently measure about decisions? How are decision-makers evaluated? (March & Sutton, *Organization Science*, 1997)

Cultural factors – What are the norms around uncertainty, dissent, speed, and adaptation? (Schein, 2010)

Skill distribution – Where does decision-making skill currently reside? Is it concentrated or distributed? (Hollenbeck et al., *Academy of Management Review*, 1995)

The Risk Efficacy Audit

Based on research across organizations, I've developed a structured approach to assessing current decision-making. The Risk Efficacy Audit examines six dimensions:

- **I. Calibration patterns** – How well does confidence match reality across the organization?
- **II. Information and uncertainty practices** – How is information gathered, shared, filtered, and integrated? How is uncertainty acknowledged, communicated, and managed?
- **III. Adaptation and recovery mechanisms** – How do decisions adjust as circumstances change? How are problems detected and recovered from?
- **IV. Outcome measurement** – How are outcomes measured and evaluated? Are they contextualized appropriately?
- **V. Integration capacity** – How well are different decision aspects coordinated?
- **VI. Learning systems** – How does the organization learn from decision outcomes and processes?

The audit uses multiple methods: document analysis, decision process observation, interviews, and decision tracking. Critically, it focuses on processes, not just outcomes, and on patterns, not just individual decisions.

Case Study: A Quantitative Trading Firm

As an illustrative example, consider how one organization would implement risk efficacy measurement. A quantitative trading firm with 150 employees had consistently strong returns but experienced periodic large losses that worried leadership. Traditional risk metrics (VaR, Sharpe ratios) didn't predict these losses. The firm decided to implement risk efficacy assessment.

Phase 1: Current State Analysis

They began by analyzing past decisions that led to losses versus those that led to gains. They found patterns:

- Loss decisions showed overconfidence, poor uncertainty quantification, and failure to update as conditions changed
- Gain decisions showed better calibration, explicit scenario planning, and continuous adjustment
- The firm's culture rewarded conviction and punished expressions of doubt

Phase 2: Pilot Implementation

They selected three trading teams for a six-month pilot:

- Traders kept decision journals documenting reasoning, confidence levels, and key uncertainties
- Weekly reviews focused on decision processes, not just P&L
- New metrics tracked calibration (confidence vs. accuracy) and adaptation speed

Phase 3: Initial Findings

After six months:

- Pilot teams showed 40% fewer large losses than control teams
- The best predictors of success weren't traditional metrics but process measures (quality of uncertainty quantification, frequency of belief updating)
- Cultural resistance was significant—traders initially saw process tracking as bureaucratic

Phase 4: Refinement and Scale

Based on pilot learning, they:

- Simplified tracking to focus on highest-impact decisions
- Integrated process metrics with existing performance systems
- Trained managers in giving feedback on decision processes
- Celebrated examples where good processes led to avoiding losses (not just making gains)

Results after two years:

- Large loss events decreased by 60%
- Risk-adjusted returns improved slightly
- Cultural shift: expressions of uncertainty became more acceptable
- Unexpected benefit: better knowledge sharing as decision patterns became visible

This case illustrates several implementation principles: start with understanding current state, pilot before scaling, measure what matters (not just what's easy), and expect cultural resistance.

The Implementation Framework

Based on research and case studies, I propose a framework for implementing risk efficacy measurement:

Phase 1: Foundation (Months 1-3)

- **Leadership alignment** – Ensure key leaders understand and support the initiative
- **Current state assessment** – Conduct Risk Efficacy Audit
- **Goal setting** – Define what success looks like, both quantitatively and qualitatively
- **Pilot selection** – Choose 1-2 teams or decision types for initial implementation

Phase 2: Pilot (Months 4-9)

- **Measurement design** – Create simple tracking for key risk efficacy dimensions
- **Training** – Train pilot teams on new practices and metrics
- **Implementation** – Launch pilot with regular check-ins
- **Learning and adjustment** – Collect feedback, adjust approach

Phase 3: Refinement (Months 10-12)

- **Pilot evaluation** – Assess what worked and what didn't
- **Framework refinement** – Adjust measurement and practices based on learning
- **Scaling planning** – Plan broader implementation

Phase 4: Integration (Year 2+)

- **Broader implementation** – Scale to more teams/decisions
- **System integration** – Embed risk efficacy into existing systems (performance management, planning, etc.)
- **Continuous improvement** – Establish ongoing assessment and refinement

Measurement Design Principles

Effective measurement of risk efficacy follows several research-based principles:

Minimize burden – Tracking should take less than 5% of decision-makers' time (otherwise it won't be sustained)

Focus on high-impact decisions – Not all decisions need detailed tracking; identify the 20% of decisions that drive 80% of impact

Balance quantitative and qualitative – Some aspects (calibration) lend themselves to numbers; others (integration) require narrative

Make it useful for decision-makers – Measurement should provide immediate value (better decisions, clearer thinking), not just organizational oversight

Ensure psychological safety – People won't honestly track uncertainties and mistakes if they fear punishment

Build on existing processes – Integrate with how decisions already get made rather than creating parallel processes

The Tools

Based on what works across organizations, here are practical tools for implementation:

The Decision Canvas

A one-page template that guides decision-makers through key considerations:

- What are we deciding? (Clarity of decision statement)
- What do we know? What don't we know? (Informed navigation)
- How confident are we? Why? (Calibration)
- How will we adapt if things change? (Resilience planning)
- What does success look like? How will we measure it? (Outcome intention)

The Decision Journal

A simple tracking tool where decision-makers record:

- Date and decision context
- Key information considered and uncertainties identified
- Decision and rationale
- Confidence level (0-100%) and reasoning
- Adaptation triggers and plans

- Later: What actually happened and why

The Risk Efficacy Dashboard

For organizational tracking, a dashboard showing:

- Decision quality metrics across teams
- Calibration trends over time
- Adaptation and recovery patterns
- Outcome achievement with appropriate context
- Learning from decision reviews

The Decision Review Protocol

A structured approach for reviewing decisions that focuses on process:

- What was the decision context?
- What process was followed across the four dimensions?
- What worked well in the process?
- What could be improved?
- What did we learn?
- How will we apply this learning?

Overcoming Resistance

Research on organizational change identifies common sources of resistance to decision process improvements:

Time pressure – "We don't have time for process; we need to decide now."

Perceived bureaucracy – "This is just more paperwork."

Threat to autonomy – "You're trying to standardize creativity."

Measurement anxiety – "You're going to judge me on process rather than results."

Skill gaps – "I don't know how to do what you're asking."

Effective implementation addresses these concerns:

Start with high-value, low-frequency decisions – Begin with strategic decisions that have significant impact but don't happen daily, minimizing time burden.

Co-create processes – Involve decision-makers in designing tracking and review processes.

Focus on learning, not judgment – Frame measurement as improvement tool, not evaluation tool.

Provide training and coaching – Build skills in probabilistic thinking, uncertainty communication, adaptation planning, etc.

Leader modeling – Have leaders visibly use the new processes for their own decisions.

The Cultural Shift

Implementing risk efficacy measurement requires cultural changes:

From outcomes to processes – Valuing how decisions get made, not just what results.

From certainty to probabilistic thinking – Embracing uncertainty rather than pretending it doesn't exist.

From individual genius to collective wisdom – Recognizing that the best decisions often come from integrated thinking.

From punishment to learning – Treating mistakes as learning opportunities when processes were good.

From speed to appropriate speed – Recognizing that different decisions require different paces.

This cultural shift doesn't happen through memos or training alone. It happens through consistent modeling, reinforcement, and—most importantly—through the experience that better processes lead to better outcomes.

The Implementation Paradox

Here we encounter what might be called the "implementation paradox": to implement risk efficacy measurement successfully, we need to apply risk efficacy principles to the implementation itself.

We need to:

- Integrate information about what works in similar organizations (informed navigation)
- Navigate uncertainty about how our specific organization will respond (calibration)
- Adapt our implementation based on feedback (resilience)
- Maintain focus on achieving intended results (outcome achievement)

In other words, we need to practice what we preach from day one. The implementation process becomes the first test of whether the framework works.

The Way Forward

Implementation is where frameworks meet reality. It's messy, iterative, and full of surprises. But it's also where change happens—where organizations actually become better at making decisions rather than just talking about it.

The risk efficacy framework provides principles and tools, but each organization must find its own path to implementation. What works for a quantitative trading firm differs from what works for a hospital or a technology company. The common thread is the commitment to measuring and improving decision processes, not just outcomes.

The next chapters will dive deeper into specific aspects of implementation: building measurement systems, developing decision-making skills, creating supportive cultures, and scaling across organizations. Each builds on this foundation of starting where you are, learning as you go, and staying focused on what matters: better decisions in an uncertain world.

Reflection Questions:

- 50. Consider your organization's readiness for implementing risk efficacy measurement. What would be the biggest barriers? What assets could you build on?
- 51. Think about a past attempt to improve decision-making in your organization. What worked? What didn't? What lessons would apply to implementing risk efficacy measurement?
- 52. If you were to pilot risk efficacy measurement, where would you start? What decisions or teams would be good candidates for a pilot?

Exercise: Implementation Planning

Choose one area where you'd like to improve decision-making. Develop a simple implementation plan:

- 53. Current State: What's happening now? How are decisions made? What works? What doesn't?
- 54. Goal: What would success look like? Be specific about both process and outcome improvements.
- 55. First Steps: What 2-3 small changes could you make to start improving decision processes?
- 56. Measurement: How would you know if things are improving? What would you track?
- 57. Learning: How would you learn from what works and doesn't work?
- 58. Scaling: If the initial changes work, how might they spread?

Keep this plan simple—no more than one page. The goal isn't perfection but starting.

Practice: The One-Week Experiment

For one week, try implementing one aspect of risk efficacy measurement in your own decision-making:

- Choose 2-3 significant decisions to track
- Use a simple decision journal format
- At week's end, review what you learned about your decision process
- Identify one small improvement for the following week

The goal isn't to transform your decision-making in a week, but to experience what measurement feels like and what it reveals.

Chapter 9: Building Measurement Systems

The Art of Measuring What Matters

In the early 2000s, a team of researchers at Carnegie Mellon made a discovery that changed how we think about measuring complex skills. They were studying expert software engineers—people who could design systems that worked elegantly under pressure. Traditional metrics like lines of code or bugs fixed failed to capture what made these engineers exceptional. So the researchers tried something different: they measured decision points. They tracked how engineers navigated design choices, how they handled ambiguous requirements, how they adapted when initial approaches failed. What emerged wasn't a score, but a pattern—a signature of expert thinking that was invisible to conventional metrics (Perry et al., *IEEE Transactions on Software Engineering*, 2001).

This insight applies beyond software engineering. When we try to measure decision-making quality, we face a fundamental challenge: the most important aspects are often the least visible. We can't directly observe how someone integrates information, navigates uncertainty, or calibrates confidence. We see only the outcomes—the code written, the trades made, the surgeries performed.

The risk efficacy framework offers a way through this challenge. It suggests that while we can't measure decision quality directly, we can measure its traces—the observable behaviors that indicate how decisions are being made.

The Research: What Can Be Measured

Decades of research across domains reveal that expert decision-making leaves consistent traces:

Calibration can be measured through:

- Confidence-accuracy correlation
- Prediction tracking accuracy
- Belief updating appropriateness

Informed navigation can be measured through:

- Source diversity (number and variety of information sources consulted)
- Signal-to-noise ratio (proportion of relevant to irrelevant information considered)
- Uncertainty accounting (explicit identification and addressing of unknowns)
- Integration patterns (how different pieces of information are connected)

Resilience can be measured through:

- Adaptation planning (inclusion of adaptation triggers in plans)
- Detection and response times for problems
- Resolution quality (permanent vs. temporary fixes)
- Learning capture (system changes to prevent recurrence)

Outcome achievement can be measured through:

- Intention-outcome alignment
- Time horizon consistency

- Risk-adjusted returns
- Pattern recognition across decisions

What makes these measures powerful isn't their individual precision, but their collective pattern. As psychologist Robyn Dawes noted, "The whole point of measurement is not to achieve perfect accuracy, but to achieve sufficient accuracy to make better decisions than we would without measurement" (Dawes, *Rational Choice in an Uncertain World*, 1988).

The Measurement Design Principles

Based on research across organizations, effective measurement systems for decision quality follow specific principles:

Principle 1: Measure Process, Not Just Outcomes

This is the core insight of the risk efficacy framework. Outcomes matter, but they're noisy indicators of decision quality. Process measures—how decisions are made—provide clearer signals.

Research on medical error reduction shows this principle in action. When hospitals started tracking not just patient outcomes but decision processes (whether checklists were followed, whether team communication met standards), error rates dropped significantly (Pronovost et al., *New England Journal of Medicine*, 2006). The process measures provided earlier, more actionable feedback than outcome measures alone.

Principle 2: Measure at Multiple Time Points

Decision quality isn't a single event; it's a process that unfolds over time. Effective measurement systems capture this temporal dimension.

In a study of investment decision-making, researchers found that the most predictive measures weren't of the initial decision, but of how decisions evolved as new information emerged (Muthukrishnan & Wathieu, *Journal of Consumer Research*, 2007). Decision-makers who updated their assessments appropriately as information arrived achieved better outcomes than those who made brilliant initial assessments but failed to update.

Principle 3: Balance Quantitative and Qualitative Measures

Some aspects of decision quality lend themselves to numbers (calibration scores, prediction accuracy). Others require narrative (reasoning quality, integration patterns). The best systems use both.

Research on performance assessment shows that purely quantitative measures miss important nuances, while purely qualitative measures lack comparability (Borman, *Annual Review of Psychology*, 1991). Hybrid approaches that combine numerical scores with narrative explanations provide the richest understanding.

Principle 4: Minimize Measurement Burden

If measurement takes too much time or effort, it won't be sustained. The most effective systems are lightweight, integrated into existing workflows, and provide immediate value to those being measured.

Studies of organizational measurement systems consistently find an inverse relationship between measurement burden and data quality (Meyer, 1994). When people feel overwhelmed by measurement requirements, they either rebel (refusing to comply) or comply superficially (entering meaningless data).

Principle 5: Ensure Psychological Safety

People won't honestly report uncertainties, mistakes, or doubts if they fear punishment. Measurement systems must be designed for learning, not judgment.

Amy Edmondson's research on psychological safety shows that teams that feel safe admitting errors and uncertainties learn faster and perform better (Edmondson, 1999). Measurement systems that punish vulnerability drive learning underground.

The Measurement Toolkit

Based on these principles, here are practical tools for measuring risk efficacy:

Tool 1: The Decision Log

A lightweight tracking system for individual decisions:
Format: Simple template (digital or paper) with fields for:

- Decision context (What are we deciding? Why now?)
- Information considered (Sources, key data points, assumptions, uncertainties)
- Confidence level (0-100% with reasoning)
- Adaptation triggers and plans
- Success criteria and measurement approach
- Outcome and learning (Completed later: what happened and why)

Research basis: Decision journals have been shown to improve calibration and learning across domains (Russo & Schoemaker, 1989). The key is simplicity—if it takes more than 5 minutes per significant decision, it won't be sustained.

Tool 2: The Decision Review Protocol

A structured approach for reviewing decisions in teams:
Format: Regular meetings (weekly or monthly) where teams review 1-2 significant decisions using a standard protocol:

- **Context**: What were we deciding? What constraints did we face?
- **Process**: How did we make the decision? What steps did we follow across the four dimensions?
- **Information and uncertainty**: What information did we have? What uncertainties did we acknowledge? How did we address them?
- **Calibration**: How confident were we? Was that confidence justified?
- **Adaptation and recovery**: What adaptations were planned? What adaptations were needed? How did we recover from surprises?
- **Outcome**: What happened? How does it compare to what we intended?
- **Learning**: What worked well in our process? What would we do differently?

Research basis: Structured debriefs improve team performance by 20-25% across domains (Tannenbaum & Cerasoli, *Journal of Applied Psychology*, 2013). The key is focusing on process, not blame.

Tool 3: The Calibration Dashboard

A visual display of prediction accuracy over time:
Format: Simple chart showing for each prediction:

- What was predicted (with confidence level)
- What actually happened
- The difference (calibration error)

Research basis: Regular feedback on calibration improves accuracy over time (Mellers et al., 2014). The key is tracking predictions that matter and reviewing them regularly.

Tool 4: The Uncertainty Map

A visual tool for mapping and tracking uncertainties:
Format: Two-dimensional map with axes for:

- Impact (low to high)
- Uncertainty (well-understood to unknown)

Each uncertainty is plotted as a bubble, with size representing importance and color representing status (acknowledged, quantified, planned for, resolved).
Research basis: Visual representations of complex information improve understanding and decision quality (Keller & Tergan, *Knowledge and Information Visualization*, 2005). The key is keeping it simple and actionable.

Case Study: Implementing Measurement in a Hospital System

As an illustrative example, consider how one hospital system would implement risk efficacy measurement to improve surgical outcomes:

The Problem: The hospital had good overall outcomes but experienced unpredictable complications. Traditional morbidity and mortality conferences focused on outcomes, not decision processes.

The Solution: They implemented a modified decision review protocol for surgical teams:

- **Pre-operative decision tracking**: Surgeons completed brief decision logs for complex cases, documenting key uncertainties and contingency plans.
- **Intra-operative adaptation tracking**: Anesthesia teams tracked decision points during surgery, noting when adaptations were made and why.
- **Post-operative review**: Teams reviewed not just outcomes, but decision processes using a structured protocol.

The Measures: They tracked:

- Percentage of cases with completed decision logs
- Number of uncertainties identified per case
- Frequency of appropriate intra-operative adaptations
- Calibration of pre-operative risk assessments
- Outcome patterns relative to decision quality

The Results (after 18 months):

- Surgical complications decreased by 32%
- Team communication scores improved by 45%
- Surgeons reported better preparedness for complex cases
- Unexpected finding: junior surgeons learned faster because they could see expert decision processes

Key insights from implementation:

- Start with volunteers (early adopters)
- Keep tracking minimal (initially 3-5 key data points)
- Provide immediate value (teams saw better outcomes quickly)
- Iterate based on feedback (simplified forms twice in first year)

Measurement Pitfalls and Solutions

Research and experience reveal common pitfalls in measuring decision quality:

Pitfall 1: Measuring Too Much

Problem: Organizations try to measure everything, creating measurement fatigue.
Solution: Focus on 3-5 key metrics that matter most. Use the 80/20 rule: what 20% of measures will give 80% of the insight?

Pitfall 2: Measuring the Wrong Things

Problem: Organizations measure what's easy to measure, not what matters.
Solution: Regularly review measures against decision outcomes. Are they predictive? Do they provide actionable insights?

Pitfall 3: Using Measures for Punishment

Problem: Measures become tools for evaluation rather than improvement.
Solution: Separate measurement for learning from measurement for evaluation. Create safe spaces for experimentation and failure.

Pitfall 4: Ignoring Context

Problem: Applying the same measures across different contexts.
Solution: Customize measures to decision type and context. What matters for strategic decisions differs from operational decisions.

Pitfall 5: Failing to Iterate

Problem: Measurement systems become rigid and outdated.
Solution: Regularly review and update measures. What worked initially may need adjustment as the organization learns.

The Role of Technology

Technology can support—but not replace—good measurement design:

Decision tracking platforms: Simple apps that make decision logging easy and integrated into workflows.

Prediction markets: Internal systems where employees can make and track predictions on key outcomes.

Collaboration tools: Platforms that capture decision discussions and rationale.

Analytics dashboards: Systems that aggregate and visualize decision metrics.

The key principle: technology should reduce measurement burden, not increase it. As psychologist Don Norman notes, "The real problem with the technological approach is that it doesn't solve the right problem. Often, the problem is not technology but psychology" (Norman, *The Design of Everyday Things*, 1988).

The Measurement Culture

Ultimately, measurement systems work only within supportive cultures:

Learning orientation: The organization values learning and improvement over proving correctness.

Psychological safety: People feel safe being honest about uncertainties and mistakes.

Transparency: Decision processes and metrics are visible, not hidden.

Curiosity: There's genuine interest in understanding how decisions work, not just judging them.

Patience: Improvement takes time; there's tolerance for experimentation and iteration.

Research on organizational learning shows that these cultural factors matter more than specific measurement tools (Argyris & Schön, *Organizational Learning*, 1978). The best measurement system will fail in a culture of blame and secrecy.

The Measurement Journey

Implementing decision quality measurement is a journey, not a destination. It involves:

- **Starting simple**: Begin with 1-2 measures that matter.

- **Learning and adapting**: Use measurement to learn what works, then adapt.
- **Building gradually**: Add measures as the organization develops measurement maturity.
- **Integrating into culture**: Make measurement part of how the organization works, not an add-on.

The goal isn't perfect measurement, but better measurement—measurement that provides enough insight to improve decisions incrementally over time.

The Way Forward

Measurement is how we make the invisible visible. It's how we transform decision-making from an art to a discipline—something that can be understood, improved, and taught.

The risk efficacy framework provides a roadmap for what to measure. The tools and principles in this chapter provide guidance for how to measure it. But the real work happens in practice—in the daily decisions where measurement meets reality.

The next chapter will explore how to use these measurements to develop decision-making skills—how to move from measuring what is to building what could be.

Reflection Questions:

- 59. Consider your current measurement practices around decisions. What do you measure? How does it help or hinder good decision-making?
- 60. If you were to implement one new measure of decision quality, what would it be? Why that one?
- 61. What cultural changes would be needed in your organization to support better decision measurement?

Exercise: Measurement Design

Choose one type of decision in your organization (hiring, project approval, resource allocation, etc.). Design a simple measurement approach:

- 62. **What matters**: What 2-3 aspects of decision quality are most important for this type of decision?
- 63. **How to measure**: How could you measure each aspect with minimal burden?
- 64. **How to use**: How would you use the measurements to improve decisions?
- 65. **How to iterate**: How would you learn from the measurements and improve them?

Keep your design to one page. The goal is feasibility, not perfection.

Practice: One-Month Measurement Experiment

For one month, implement simple measurement for your own decisions:

- Choose 3-5 significant decisions to track
- Use a simple decision log (paper or digital)
- At month's end, review what the measurements reveal
- Identify one insight about your decision process
- Plan one small improvement based on that insight

The goal is to experience measurement firsthand—its benefits, its challenges, and its potential.

Chapter 10: Recognizing Merit in Uncertainty

The Problem of Recognition

In 2016, a team of organizational researchers published a study that should have been alarming to anyone who believes in meritocracy. They followed 1,800 executives over five years, tracking promotions, compensation, and project assignments (Carnahan & Greenwood, *Strategic Management Journal*, 2018). The finding wasn't about overt discrimination. Rather, they discovered something subtler: executives who took calculated, well-managed risks were promoted at the same rate as those who took reckless, poorly-managed risks—as long as both produced good outcomes. The system couldn't tell the difference between skill and luck, between calculated navigation and reckless gambling.

This problem—the inability to distinguish between different *kinds* of success—pervades organizations. We celebrate outcomes while remaining blind to processes. We reward luck while calling it skill. And in doing so, we systematically misallocate recognition, promotion, and opportunity.

The risk efficacy framework offers a way out of this trap. By measuring decision processes rather than just outcomes, we can finally recognize true merit—especially the kind that often goes unnoticed.

The Research: What Gets Noticed (and What Doesn't)

Studies across domains reveal consistent patterns in what recognition systems capture and what they miss:

Confidence over calibration – People who express high confidence are rated as more competent, even when their accuracy is lower (Anderson et al., 2012). The confident voice gets heard, while the calibrated voice gets dismissed as uncertain.

Decisiveness over deliberation – Quick decisions are interpreted as leadership, while deliberate consideration is interpreted as hesitation (Klein, 2009). The fast decider gets promoted; the thoughtful decider gets told to "be more decisive."

Consistency over adaptation – Sticking to plans is interpreted as commitment, while adapting plans is interpreted as inconsistency (Weick & Sutcliffe, 2007). The rigid executor gets praised; the flexible adapter gets criticized.

Boldness over calculation – Taking big risks is interpreted as courage, while managing risks carefully is interpreted as caution (March & Shapira, 1992). The reckless risk-taker gets celebrated when lucky; the careful risk-manager gets overlooked.

These patterns create systematic biases in who gets recognized as excellent. They favor one approach to decision-making—confident, decisive, consistent, bold—over others that may be equally or more effective.

The Gender Dimension

Research reveals particularly troubling patterns when these biases intersect with gender. Multiple studies show:

Women are more likely to:

- Express calibrated confidence rather than overconfidence (Brescoll, 2012)
- Consider multiple alternatives before deciding (Galinsky et al., 2003)
- Adapt plans based on new information (Eagly & Johnson, 1990)

- Manage risks carefully rather than take bold risks (Byrnes et al., 1999)

Yet these very tendencies are often misinterpreted:

- Calibrated confidence is interpreted as lack of confidence
- Considering alternatives is interpreted as indecisiveness
- Adapting plans is interpreted as inconsistency
- Risk management is interpreted as excessive caution

The result: women are systematically undervalued in recognition systems that reward overconfidence, quick decisions, rigid execution, and bold risk-taking (Correll, 2017). This isn't necessarily intentional discrimination; it's the consequence of recognition systems that measure the wrong things.

The Risk Efficacy Solution

The risk efficacy framework addresses these biases by measuring what matters:

Instead of confidence alone, measure calibration – How well does someone's confidence match their accuracy? This distinguishes between well-earned confidence and empty certainty.

Instead of decisiveness alone, measure appropriate speed – How well does someone match decision pace to decision context? This distinguishes between appropriate deliberation and problematic delay.

Instead of consistency alone, measure resilience – How well does someone adapt when circumstances change and recover when problems occur? This distinguishes between stubbornness and intelligent flexibility.

Instead of boldness alone, measure calculated risk-taking – How well does someone navigate uncertainty while accounting for risks? This distinguishes between recklessness and informed navigation.

Instead of outcomes alone, measure outcome achievement in context – How well does someone achieve intended results across appropriate timeframes, with appropriate risk adjustment?

By measuring these dimensions, we can recognize excellence in all its forms—not just the loud, fast, bold pattern that traditional systems favor.

Case Study: A Technology Company's Promotion Problem

As an illustrative example, consider a technology company struggling with gender equity in senior leadership. Women comprised 45% of mid-level managers but only 20% of vice presidents. The company's promotion system relied on:

- Project outcomes (did projects succeed?)
- Manager evaluations (were they seen as "leadership material"?)
- Peer feedback (were they seen as "confident" and "decisive"?)

An analysis revealed patterns:

- Women received feedback about needing to be "more confident" and "more decisive"
- Men who took bold risks that paid off were fast-tracked
- Women who managed projects carefully with good outcomes were told to "take more risks"
- 80% of promotions went to managers rated "highly confident" by peers

The company implemented risk efficacy measurement alongside their traditional promotion process. For six months, they tracked:

- Calibration scores (confidence vs. accuracy on project predictions)
- Decision journals for key project decisions
- Adaptation patterns during project execution

- Uncertainty management in risk planning
- Outcome achievement across appropriate timeframes

The findings were revealing:

- Women showed better calibration than men (their confidence more closely matched reality)
- Men were more likely to express high confidence regardless of accuracy
- Women documented more thorough decision processes and considered more alternatives
- Men were more likely to stick to initial plans even when circumstances changed
- Women's projects showed better long-term outcomes despite sometimes slower starts

Most importantly: when promotion committees saw the risk efficacy data alongside traditional metrics, their decisions changed. Managers who showed strong calibration, thorough decision processes, intelligent adaptation, and good long-term outcomes—disproportionately women—were recognized as excellent even when their traditional evaluations contained phrases like "needs to be more confident."

After two years of using risk efficacy data in promotions:

- Women's representation in vice president roles increased from 20% to 35%
- Project failure rates decreased by 25%
- Employee surveys showed increased perception of fairness in promotions
- Long-term project success rates improved

The system didn't favor women; it simply stopped systematically disadvantaging a particular approach to decision-making that happened to be more common among women.

The Components of Fair Recognition

Based on research and case studies, fair recognition systems share several components:

1. Multi-Dimensional Measurement

Traditional systems often rely on single dimensions (outcomes, confidence, speed). Fair systems measure multiple dimensions of decision quality, recognizing that excellence comes in different forms.

Research on performance assessment shows that multi-dimensional systems reduce bias and improve accuracy (Murphy & Cleveland, *Performance Appraisal*, 1995). When we measure only what's easy to measure or what matches our stereotypes, we miss important aspects of performance.

2. Process Visibility

In traditional systems, decision processes are invisible; only outcomes are visible. Fair systems make processes visible through tools like decision journals, review protocols, and calibration tracking.

Studies of high-reliability organizations show that process visibility improves both performance and fairness (Weick & Sutcliffe, 2007). When everyone can see how decisions are made, it's harder for biases to operate unnoticed.

3. Calibration Against Reality

Traditional systems often measure against subjective standards (manager opinions, peer perceptions). Fair systems measure against objective reality (prediction accuracy, outcome calibration).

Research on bias reduction shows that anchoring evaluations in objective reality reduces the influence of stereotypes (Greenwald & Banaji, *Psychological Review*, 1995). When we measure whether predictions come true rather than whether someone "sounds confident," we bypass many biases.

4. Contextual Understanding

Traditional systems often apply the same standards across contexts. Fair systems recognize that different situations require different approaches.

Studies of expert decision-making show that adaptability—matching approach to context—is a hallmark of expertise (Klein, 2009). Recognizing this requires understanding context, not just evaluating decisions in isolation.

5. Time Horizon Awareness

Traditional systems often reward short-term results. Fair systems evaluate outcomes across appropriate time horizons.

Research on temporal discounting shows that organizations naturally overweight short-term results (Laverty, *Organization Science*, 1996). Fair recognition systems counter this bias by valuing long-term success appropriately.

Implementing Fair Recognition

Based on what works in organizations, here are steps for implementing risk-efficacy-based recognition:

Step 1: Baseline Assessment

Before changing recognition systems, understand current patterns:

- Who gets recognized and why?
- What metrics are used?
- What biases exist in current evaluations?
- How do recognition patterns correlate with demographic factors?

This assessment should include both quantitative analysis (promotion rates, compensation patterns) and qualitative analysis (evaluation language, feedback patterns).

Step 2: Pilot Implementation

Start with a pilot in one department or for one type of decision (promotions, project assignments, bonuses). Implement risk efficacy measurement alongside traditional systems.

The pilot should:

- Be voluntary initially (early adopters first)
- Include training on new metrics and processes
- Have clear evaluation criteria
- Include mechanisms for feedback and adjustment

Step 3: Parallel Tracking

Run new and old systems in parallel for 6-12 months. Compare results:

- Do the systems identify different people as excellent?
- What does each system miss that the other catches?
- How do employees perceive the fairness of each system?

Parallel tracking reduces resistance by allowing comparison rather than immediate replacement.

Step 4: Integration and Scaling

Based on pilot results, integrate risk efficacy measures into formal recognition systems. This might involve:

- Adding decision quality metrics to performance evaluations
- Training managers on interpreting risk efficacy data
- Adjusting promotion and compensation criteria
- Creating transparency about how decisions are made

The Tools for Fair Recognition
Several tools support risk-efficacy-based recognition:

The Decision Quality Portfolio

For each individual, a portfolio showing:

- Calibration scores over time
- Decision journal samples
- Adaptation and recovery patterns
- Outcome achievement with appropriate context
- Integration examples across dimensions

This portfolio provides a richer, more nuanced picture than traditional evaluations.

The Comparative Calibration Dashboard

For teams or departments, a dashboard showing:

- Calibration distributions
- Decision process quality metrics
- Adaptation and recovery effectiveness
- Outcome patterns across timeframes

- Recognition patterns against these metrics

This helps identify whether recognition aligns with decision quality.

The Recognition Audit Protocol

A regular audit process that examines:

- Who got recognized and why
- How recognition decisions were made
- Whether risk efficacy data was considered
- Whether biases might have influenced decisions
- How recognition patterns correlate with demographic factors

Regular audits maintain system integrity over time.

Overcoming Resistance

Implementing fair recognition systems faces predictable resistance:

"This is too subjective" – Actually, measuring decision processes is often more objective than measuring outcomes (which include luck) or perceptions (which include bias).

"This takes too much time" – The time spent on unfair recognition systems (appeals, turnover, disengagement) often exceeds the time needed for fair systems.

"We'll promote the wrong people" – The real risk is promoting the wrong people under current systems—those who are lucky or confident rather than skilled.

"This reduces accountability" – Actually, it increases accountability by making decision processes visible and measurable.

"This is just another HR fad" – Unlike many fads, risk efficacy measurement is grounded in decades of research across multiple disciplines.

Addressing these concerns requires data, patience, and leadership commitment. Early wins—showing how the new system catches excellence that the old system missed—build momentum.

The Broader Implications

Fair recognition systems based on risk efficacy have implications beyond individual organizations:

Meritocracy realized – True meritocracy requires accurate measurement of merit. Risk efficacy provides that measurement where it matters most: in uncertain, complex decisions.

Diversity and inclusion – By recognizing different approaches to excellence, these systems naturally create more diverse leadership—not through quotas or preferences, but through accurate measurement.

Innovation and resilience – Organizations that recognize calculated risk-taking and intelligent adaptation become more innovative and resilient.

Psychological safety – When people are evaluated on their decision processes rather than just outcomes, they feel safer taking appropriate risks and admitting uncertainties.

Learning organizations – Fair recognition systems create feedback loops that accelerate organizational learning about what works in decision-making.

Societal impact – As more organizations adopt fair recognition systems, they create models that can be adopted by educational institutions, government agencies, and other societal institutions.

The Limits of Measurement

It's important to acknowledge what risk efficacy measurement cannot do:

It doesn't eliminate all bias – All measurement systems can be biased. The goal is reduction, not elimination.

It doesn't capture everything – Some aspects of excellence (creativity, empathy, vision) fall outside decision quality measurement.

It requires interpretation – Data doesn't speak for itself; it requires thoughtful interpretation in context.

It evolves over time – As organizations learn, their measurement systems need to evolve.

It's not a substitute for judgment – Measurement informs judgment; it doesn't replace it.

The goal isn't perfect measurement, but better measurement—measurement that recognizes more of what matters and less of what doesn't.

The Way Forward

Recognition is how organizations signal what they value. When we recognize confidence over calibration, decisiveness over deliberation, consistency over adaptation, boldness over calculation, and short-term outcomes over long-term value, we're saying those things matter most. We're shaping behavior in those directions.

The risk efficacy framework offers a different signal: we value thoughtful navigation of uncertainty. We value decisions that are well-made, not just successful. We value learning and adaptation. We value accurate self-assessment. We value calculated risk-taking.

Changing recognition systems is one of the most powerful ways to change organizational behavior. It's also one of the most difficult, because it challenges entrenched patterns and power structures.

But the alternative—continuing to recognize luck as skill, overconfidence as leadership, recklessness as courage—is increasingly untenable in complex, uncertain environments. Organizations that can't distinguish between different kinds of success will eventually promote the wrong people into the wrong roles, with predictable consequences.

The next chapter will explore how to build these recognition systems into the fabric of organizations—how to move from pilot projects to cultural change, from measurement to mindset.

Reflection Questions:

- 66. Consider your organization's recognition systems. What do they currently recognize? What do they miss?
- 67. Think about someone in your organization whose excellence might be invisible to current recognition systems. How would risk efficacy measurement make their excellence visible?
- 68. What would be the biggest barriers to implementing risk-efficacy-based recognition in your organization? How might you address them?

Exercise: Recognition System Audit
Conduct a simple audit of your organization's recognition systems:

- 69. **What gets recognized**: List the last 5 people recognized (promoted, awarded, praised) and why.
- 70. **Measurement analysis**: What was measured in those recognitions? Outcomes? Perceptions? Behaviors?
- 71. **Pattern analysis**: Are there patterns in who gets recognized? Do certain approaches or styles dominate?
- 72. **Missing excellence**: Can you identify someone whose excellence might not be captured by current systems?
- 73. **Risk efficacy alternative**: How might risk efficacy measurement change those recognition decisions?

Based on this analysis, identify one small change you could make to recognition processes.

Practice: Alternative Recognition
For one month, practice recognizing people differently:

- When you see good outcomes, ask about the decision process that led to them
- When someone expresses calibrated confidence, recognize it as a strength
- When someone adapts intelligently to changing circumstances, acknowledge it

- When someone manages risks carefully, celebrate it as skill rather than caution
- When someone achieves good long-term results, recognize them even if short-term results were modest

At month's end, reflect on what you noticed. Did you see excellence you might have missed before? How did people respond to this different kind of recognition?

Chapter 11: Cultivating a Culture of Risk Efficacy

T he Soil in Which Excellence Grows
In the early 2000s, NASA conducted a study that would change how we think about organizational excellence. They weren't studying rockets or space stations, but culture. After the Columbia disaster, investigators found that the technical failure—foam striking the wing—wasn't the fundamental problem. The fundamental problem was cultural: engineers had expressed concerns about foam shedding for years, but the organization had developed what the investigation called "normalized deviance"—a culture where anomalies became accepted until they became expected, and where dissenting voices were systematically marginalized (Columbia Accident Investigation Board, 2003).

This pattern appears across domains. In finance, firms develop cultures where risk-taking is celebrated and risk management is seen as bureaucratic. In medicine, some departments develop cultures where certainty is expected and uncertainty is hidden. In technology, companies develop cultures where speed is valued over deliberation.

Culture isn't something an organization has; it's something an organization is. It's the collection of shared assumptions, unspoken rules, and implicit values that shape how people think, decide, and act.

And when it comes to decision-making, culture is the invisible hand that guides the visible choices.

The Research: Culture as Decision Infrastructure

Studies of organizational culture reveal that it operates as a kind of decision infrastructure—shaping what information gets noticed, how uncertainty gets handled, when adaptation occurs, and how confidence gets expressed.

In a landmark study of high-reliability organizations—aircraft carriers, nuclear power plants, air traffic control—researchers found that these organizations shared cultural characteristics that enabled excellent decision-making under pressure (Weick & Sutcliffe, 2007):

- **Preoccupation with failure** – Treating near-misses as system failures rather than successes
- **Reluctance to simplify** – Resisting easy explanations and seeking multiple perspectives
- **Sensitivity to operations** – Maintaining awareness of front-line realities
- **Commitment to resilience** – Building capacity to bounce back from unexpected events
- **Deference to expertise** – Following authority of knowledge rather than hierarchy

These cultural characteristics didn't emerge accidentally. They were deliberately cultivated through leadership actions, system designs, and daily practices.

Similarly, research on psychological safety—the belief that one can speak up without risk of punishment or humiliation—shows that it's a cultural condition that enables better decision-making (Edmondson, 1999). Teams with high psychological safety:

- Admit mistakes and uncertainties more readily
- Share diverse perspectives more openly

- Challenge assumptions more effectively
- Learn from failures more systematically

Culture shapes decision-making at a fundamental level. As anthropologist Clifford Geertz observed, "Culture is the stories we tell ourselves about ourselves" (Geertz, *The Interpretation of Cultures*, 1973). The stories organizations tell—about success, about failure, about what gets rewarded and punished—shape how people make decisions long before any individual choice is made.

The Challenge of Cultural Change

Changing decision-making culture is notoriously difficult. Research on organizational change suggests several reasons:

Culture is self-reinforcing – Cultural norms create behaviors that reinforce those norms, creating feedback loops that resist change (Schein, 2010). A culture that rewards overconfidence will attract and promote overconfident people, who will then reinforce the culture of overconfidence.

Culture operates implicitly – Much of culture exists below the level of conscious awareness, in unspoken assumptions and automatic behaviors (Argyris, 1990). People follow cultural rules without realizing they're following rules.

Culture change requires consistency – Inconsistent signals (leaders saying one thing but doing another) reinforce existing culture rather than creating new culture (Simons, 1995). Culture notices what you do, not just what you say.

Culture change takes time – Cultural norms develop over years and change over years, not months (Kotter, *Leading Change*, 1996). Quick fixes don't work.

Despite these challenges, cultural change is possible. Research points to specific levers that can shift decision-making culture over time.

The Levers of Cultural Change

Based on research across organizations, I've identified five levers for cultivating a culture of risk efficacy:

Lever 1: Leadership Modeling

Culture watches what leaders do, not what they say. When leaders model risk efficacy behaviors—acknowledging uncertainty, showing calibrated confidence, adapting publicly, making their decision processes transparent—they send powerful signals about what's valued.

Research on leadership and culture shows that leader behaviors account for up to 70% of the variance in psychological safety and learning behavior in teams (Edmondson, 2018). When leaders admit mistakes, ask for help, and show curiosity, they create permission for others to do the same.

Lever 2: Systems and Processes

Culture lives in systems. Promotion criteria, performance metrics, meeting structures, decision protocols—these systems encode cultural values in concrete form.

Studies of organizational design show that systems shape behavior more powerfully than speeches or training (Pfeffer & Sutton, 2000). When promotion systems reward calibrated confidence rather than overconfidence, behavior changes. When meeting protocols require explicit uncertainty assessment, thinking changes.

Lever 3: Stories and Symbols

Culture communicates through stories—the tales told about heroes and failures, the examples held up as models, the language used to describe success and failure.

Research on organizational storytelling shows that stories are more memorable and influential than policies or data (Boje, *Narrative Methods for Organizational & Communication Research*, 2001). Stories about someone who avoided disaster by speaking up about uncertainty, or about a team that succeeded through intelligent adaptation, shape cultural norms more effectively than any rule.

Lever 4: Skills and Development

Culture requires capability. People can't practice risk efficacy behaviors they don't understand or can't execute. Training in probabilistic thinking, uncertainty communication, decision journaling, and calibration tracking builds the skills needed for a risk efficacy culture.

Studies of expertise development show that skill-building must be paired with cultural support to be effective (Ericsson et al., 1993). Skills without cultural permission go unused; culture without skills remains aspirational.

Lever 5: Measurement and Feedback

Culture responds to what gets measured. When organizations measure decision processes—calibration, informed navigation, resilience, outcome achievement in context—they signal that these things matter.

Research on performance measurement shows that measurement focuses attention (Meyer, 1994). What gets measured gets discussed, gets improved, and eventually gets valued. The act of measuring decision quality makes it culturally salient.

Case Study: Transforming a Surgical Department

As an illustrative example, consider how one hospital would transform its surgical department's culture over three years:

Initial State:

- High-pressure environment where certainty was expected
- Near-misses were rarely discussed
- Senior surgeons rarely expressed uncertainty
- Junior staff hesitated to voice concerns
- Outcomes were good but complications were higher than benchmark

Interventions:

- **Leadership modeling**: Department chair began pre-operative briefings by stating "Here's what I'm uncertain about in this case." She publicly changed her mind when presented with new information.
- **System changes**: Implemented structured decision protocols for complex cases, requiring explicit uncertainty assessment and contingency planning. Changed morbidity and mortality conferences to focus on decision processes, not just outcomes.
- **Storytelling**: Collected and shared stories of near-misses caught by junior staff speaking up, of adaptations that saved patients, of calibrated confidence proving more accurate than certainty.
- **Skill building**: Trained all staff in probabilistic thinking, uncertainty communication, and decision journaling. Created simulation scenarios focused on decision processes under uncertainty.
- **Measurement**: Tracked decision quality metrics alongside patient outcomes. Shared department-level calibration scores and adaptation patterns.

Results after three years:

- Surgical complications decreased by 40%
- Staff surveys showed psychological safety increased from 35th to 85th percentile

- Junior staff speaking up increased 300%
- Unexpected benefit: teaching evaluations improved as decision processes became more transparent

Key insight: The cultural change wasn't one intervention but the integration of all five levers, consistently applied over time.

The Role of Diversity

Research reveals an important connection between diversity and decision-making culture. Diverse teams—in gender, background, experience, thinking style—create natural checks against cultural drift toward overconfidence and groupthink.

Studies show that diverse teams:

- Consider more alternatives (Page, 2007)
- Catch more errors (Woolley et al., 2010)
- Are less likely to fall into confirmation bias (Nemeth, *Minority Influence*, 1986)
- Show better calibration on complex tasks (Mellers et al., 2014)

But diversity only improves decision-making in cultures that value different perspectives. In cultures that value conformity or certainty, diversity can actually increase conflict without improving decisions (Ely & Thomas, *Harvard Business Review*, 2001).

Cultivating a risk efficacy culture creates the conditions for diversity to improve decision-making. When uncertainty is acknowledged, different perspectives become valuable rather than threatening. When adaptation is valued, diverse approaches become assets rather than liabilities. When calibration is measured, overconfidence from homogeneous groups becomes visible rather than rewarded.

The Architecture of a Risk Efficacy Culture

Based on research and case studies, here are the architectural elements of a risk efficacy culture:

Foundational Beliefs

- **Uncertainty is inevitable** – Not something to be eliminated but navigated
- **Process matters** – How decisions are made matters as much as what decisions are made
- **Learning is continuous** – Every decision is an opportunity to learn and improve
- **Dissent is valuable** – Different perspectives improve decision quality
- **Adaptation is strength** – Changing course based on new information is wisdom, not weakness
- **Calibration is measurable** – Confidence should match reality, and we can measure whether it does

Behavioral Norms

- **Express calibrated confidence** – "I'm 70% confident" rather than "I'm sure"
- **Acknowledge uncertainty explicitly** – "Here's what I don't know"
- **Consider multiple alternatives** – "What else could we do?"
- **Update beliefs with evidence** – "New information changes my thinking"
- **Make thinking visible** – "Here's how I'm reasoning about this"
- **Plan for adaptation** – "Here's how we'll adjust if things change"
- **Learn from outcomes** – "What can we learn from what happened?"

Structural Supports

- **Decision quality metrics** – Measuring process, not just outcomes
- **Psychological safety mechanisms** – Ways to speak up without fear
- **Learning rituals** – Regular reviews focused on process improvement
- **Adaptation protocols** – Clear processes for changing course
- **Transparency systems** – Making decisions and their reasoning visible
- **Calibration feedback** – Regular feedback on prediction accuracy

Leadership Practices

- **Model vulnerability** – Leaders show uncertainty and admit mistakes
- **Reward process excellence** – Recognize good decision-making even when outcomes are poor
- **Create safety for dissent** – Actively seek and value different perspectives
- **Maintain strategic patience** – Allow time for deliberation when needed
- **Practice consistent messaging** – Align words, actions, and systems
- **Measure what matters** – Implement risk efficacy measurement

The Journey of Cultural Change

Cultivating a risk efficacy culture is a journey, not a destination. Research suggests it typically follows stages:

Stage 1: Awareness (Months 1-6)

- Recognizing current cultural patterns
- Understanding the costs of current patterns
- Building shared language about decision quality
- Identifying early adopters and champions

Stage 2: Experimentation (Months 7-18)

- Piloting new practices in safe contexts
- Testing measurement approaches
- Learning what works in your specific context
- Building early success stories

Stage 3: Integration (Months 19-36)

- Scaling successful practices
- Aligning systems with new values
- Developing internal expertise
- Addressing cultural resistance

Stage 4: Sustainability (Year 4+)

- New practices become habitual
- Decision quality becomes instinctive
- Culture becomes self-reinforcing
- Continuous improvement becomes routine

This journey isn't linear; organizations often move back and forth between stages. The key is maintaining momentum through consistent leadership and measurable progress.

The Challenges Ahead
Cultivating a risk efficacy culture faces predictable challenges:

The certainty trap – In times of stress, organizations often revert to demanding certainty rather than navigating uncertainty skillfully.

The speed trap – Under pressure, deliberation feels like delay, even when it's necessary.

The consistency trap – Adaptation looks like inconsistency, even when it's intelligent.

The confidence trap – Overconfidence feels like leadership, even when it's dangerous.

The outcome trap – Good outcomes reinforce poor processes, making learning difficult.

The measurement trap – What gets measured gets done, but we often measure the wrong things.

These challenges aren't reasons to avoid cultural change; they're reasons to approach it systematically, with awareness of the natural tendencies that must be countered.

The Cultural Dividend

Organizations that cultivate risk efficacy cultures gain what might be called a "cultural dividend":

Better decisions – Across the organization, not just in isolated pockets

Faster learning – From both successes and failures

Increased resilience – Ability to adapt to unexpected challenges

Improved talent attraction and retention – People want to work where their thinking is valued

Enhanced innovation – Psychological safety enables experimentation

Reduced risk – Early warning signals get noticed and addressed

Fairer recognition – Excellence is recognized wherever it appears, not just in certain styles

Stronger diversity and inclusion – Different approaches are valued, not just tolerated

Perhaps most importantly, these organizations become what psychologist Carol Dweck calls "growth mindset" organizations—focused on development rather than proving fixed abilities (Dweck, 2006). They become learning organisms rather than executing machines.

The Way Forward

Culture is the ultimate decision-making system. It operates in the background of every choice, shaping what gets noticed, how information gets processed, when adaptation occurs, and how confidence gets expressed.

Changing culture is difficult work—the work of years, not months. It requires consistent leadership, aligned systems, skill development, and patient measurement. But it's work that pays compounding returns, as each improvement in decision-making culture makes further improvement easier.

The organizations that do this work—that deliberately cultivate cultures of risk efficacy—will navigate uncertainty more skillfully, make better decisions more consistently, and develop the kind of wisdom that can't be captured in any framework or metric alone.

They'll become something rare and valuable: organizations that are as good at thinking as they are at doing.

Reflection Questions:

- 74. Consider your organization's current decision-making culture. What are its strengths? What are its weaknesses?
- 75. Which of the five levers (leadership modeling, systems, stories, skills, measurement) would be most powerful for changing your organization's decision-making culture? Why?
- 76. What would be the biggest barriers to cultural change in your organization? How might you address them?

Exercise: Cultural Assessment

Assess your organization's decision-making culture using these questions:

- 77. **Uncertainty handling**: How comfortable are people expressing uncertainty? What happens when someone says "I don't know"?
- 78. **Decision process**: How much attention is paid to how decisions are made versus what decisions are made?
- 79. **Adaptation**: How is changing course viewed? Is it seen as weakness or intelligence?
- 80. **Calibration**: What's valued more: calibrated confidence or certainty?
- 81. **Learning**: How does the organization learn from decisions? From successes? From failures?
- 82. **Psychological safety**: Do people feel safe expressing dissent, admitting mistakes, or asking for help?

Based on your assessment, identify one aspect of culture you'd like to strengthen.

Practice: Cultural Intervention

Choose one small way to influence your team or organization's decision-making culture this month:

- Model one risk efficacy behavior consistently (e.g., expressing calibrated confidence)
- Change one meeting protocol to focus more on process (e.g., start with uncertainty assessment)
- Share one story that illustrates risk efficacy in action
- Provide one piece of training on a risk efficacy skill
- Implement one simple measurement of decision quality

At month's end, reflect on what changed. What resistance did you encounter? What support did you find? What would you do differently next time?

Chapter 12: Scaling the Architecture

The Paradox of Scale

There's a peculiar pattern in how good ideas grow within organizations: the clearer and more effective they are in a small team, the more they tend to distort as they spread. What began as a nuanced understanding of calibrated confidence becomes, three departments later, a simplistic rule about "expressing certainty." What started as thoughtful uncertainty navigation becomes, in another division, bureaucratic risk-aversion. The signal degrades as it travels.

This isn't just poor communication. It's a fundamental property of complex systems. In 1973, the biologist Robert May published a paper that would eventually win him a Fields Medal, though its subject was neither mathematics nor biology in the traditional sense. He demonstrated mathematically that as ecosystems grow more complex—as they add more species, more interactions, more feedback loops—they become more fragile, not more robust (*Nature*, 1973). The very connections that create resilience at small scale can create fragility at large scale.

Organizations face a similar paradox. The decision-making practices that make a team exceptional can, when scaled without adaptation, make an organization rigid. The cultural norms that enable psychological safety in a department can, when imposed uniformly, create resistance across divisions. Scale changes everything—not just quantitatively (more people, more decisions) but qualitatively (different kinds of problems, different coordination challenges).

The Research: What Changes with Scale

Studies of organizational scaling reveal predictable shifts in decision-making:

Information flow distorts – As organizations grow, information doesn't just travel farther; it changes form. Frontline insights become summarized, summarized insights become bullet points, bullet points become metrics. What started as a nuanced understanding of customer pain becomes, by the time it reaches executives, a single Net Promoter Score. Research on information distortion in hierarchies shows that bad news gets softened by about 20% with each layer it travels upward (O'Reilly, *Journal of Applied Psychology*, 1980).

Decision rights blur – In small teams, everyone knows who decides what. In large organizations, decision authority becomes ambiguous, contested, or bureaucratic. Studies of decision paralysis in growing companies show that the number of people involved in decisions increases exponentially with organizational size, while decision quality plateaus then declines (Nutt, *Administrative Science Quarterly*, 1999).

Cultural coherence fragments – What feels like "how we do things here" in a fifty-person company becomes "how they do things in that department" in a five-thousand-person organization. Research on subcultures shows that large organizations inevitably develop multiple, sometimes conflicting, cultural norms (Schein, 2010). The engineering team's culture of rigorous debate clashes with the sales team's culture of optimistic forecasting.

Feedback loops elongate – In a small team, you see the consequences of your decisions quickly. In a large organization, cause and effect separate in time and space. The strategic decision made in Q1 manifests as operational problems in Q3, by which time the decision-makers have moved on to other roles. Studies of organizational learning show that feedback delay is one of the biggest barriers to improvement in large systems (Sterman, *Business Dynamics*, 2000).

Risk perception diverges – What feels like a calculated risk to the product team feels like reckless gambling to the legal team. Research on risk perception across functions shows that different departments develop literally different neural pathways for evaluating risk—finance teams activating reward centers, compliance teams activating threat centers (Kuhnen & Knutson, *Neuron*, 2005).

These aren't problems to solve but realities to navigate. Scaling risk efficacy doesn't mean making a large organization behave like a small team. It means designing systems that work at scale while preserving the core principles that work in small settings.

A Framework for Scaling

Based on research and observation across organizations that have successfully scaled decision-quality initiatives, I propose a framework with three components:

1. The Core: Principles That Don't Change

These are the non-negotiables, the ideas that must remain constant regardless of scale:

- **Process matters as much as outcome** – This can't become "outcomes matter most" at scale
- **Uncertainty must be acknowledged, not hidden** – This can't become "project confidence" at scale
- **Calibration is measurable and improvable** – This can't become "confidence is what matters" at scale
- **Adaptation is strength, not weakness** – This can't become "stick to the plan" at scale
- **Outcomes must be contextualized** – This can't become "results are all that matter" at scale

The challenge is preserving these principles while changing nearly everything else about how they're implemented.

2. The Context: What Must Change

These are the aspects that must adapt to scale:

- **Measurement granularity** – What gets measured in detail versus sampled
- **Decision categorization** – Which decisions get full risk efficacy treatment versus lighter versions
- **Communication mechanisms** – How principles and practices are explained and reinforced
- **Training approaches** – How skills are developed across large, diverse populations
- **Integration depth** – How deeply risk efficacy connects to other systems (HR, planning, etc.)

3. The Connective Tissue: What Links Core and Context

These are the mechanisms that maintain coherence while allowing adaptation:

- **Shared language** – Common terminology that means the same thing everywhere
- **Exemplars and anti-patterns** – Clear examples of what good looks like (and doesn't look like) in different contexts
- **Feedback loops** – Systems for learning what's working and what's not as practices scale
- **Adaptation protocols** – Clear processes for customizing practices to local contexts while maintaining principles

Phase 1: Assessment and Segmentation (Months 1-3)

Before scaling, understand where you're starting from. Research on successful scaling initiatives shows that organizations that skip this phase fail at about twice the rate of those that don't (Kotter, 1996).

The Scaling Assessment

Conduct a structured assessment across four dimensions:

1. Decision Typology Mapping

Not all decisions are created equal. Research on decision categorization suggests that organizations make five types of decisions, each requiring different approaches (Courtney et al., 1997):

- **Type 1: Clear-cause decisions** – Facts are known, cause-effect relationships are understood
- **Type 2: Multiple-cause decisions** – Several plausible explanations exist
- **Type 3: Uncertain-cause decisions** – Causes are unknown or unknowable
- **Type 4: Ambiguous decisions** – Not even the problem is clear
- **Type 5: Emergent decisions** – The situation is actively changing as you decide

Map where these decision types occur in your organization. Risk efficacy practices will look different for each.

2. Cultural Readiness Assessment

Different parts of your organization will be ready for different aspects of risk efficacy. Research on change readiness suggests assessing:

- Psychological safety levels (Edmondson, 1999)
- Existing decision-quality practices
- Leadership commitment and capability
- Measurement maturity
- Learning orientation

3. Infrastructure Analysis

What systems already exist that could support or hinder scaling?

- Performance management systems
- Planning and strategy processes
- Training and development programs
- Communication channels
- Technology platforms

4. Stakeholder Landscape

Who are the influencers, resistors, and amplifiers? Research on innovation diffusion shows that successful scaling requires understanding and engaging different adoption segments (Rogers, *Diffusion of Innovations*, 2003):

- Innovators (2.5%) – Will try anything new
- Early adopters (13.5%) – Respected opinion leaders
- Early majority (34%) – Need proof before adopting
- Late majority (34%) – Skeptical, adopt only under pressure
- Laggards (16%) – Resist until absolutely necessary

Segmentation Strategy

Based on your assessment, segment the organization for phased scaling:

First wave (Months 4-9): Areas with high readiness, high impact decisions, and influential early adopters. These should be your beachheads.

Second wave (Months 10-18): Areas adjacent to first-wave successes, with moderate readiness. Success in first wave creates pull for second wave.

Third wave (Months 19-30): The rest of the organization, including resistant areas. By this point, you have proof, momentum, and internal expertise.

Phase 2: Customization and Integration (Ongoing)
This is where most scaling efforts fail: they try to replicate exactly what worked in the pilot. But scale requires customization.

Customization Principles

Based on research on effective scaling:
Customize practices, not principles – How risk efficacy gets implemented can vary by department, but the core principles must remain constant.
Match rigor to decision impact – Not all decisions need full decision journals and calibration tracking. Research on decision analysis suggests matching analysis depth to decision stakes (Hammond et al., *Smart Choices*, 1999).
Adapt to cultural sub-contexts – Engineering teams may embrace probabilistic thinking but resist what they see as "touchy-feely" psychological safety practices. Sales teams may embrace adaptation but resist rigorous uncertainty quantification. Customize accordingly.
Build on existing systems – Don't create parallel processes. Integrate risk efficacy into existing meetings, reporting, planning, and review systems.

Integration Points

Research shows that initiatives integrate best when they connect to three existing systems:
1. Performance Management

- Include decision-quality metrics in performance reviews
- Train managers to give feedback on decision processes
- Align promotion criteria with risk efficacy principles

2. Planning and Strategy

- Incorporate uncertainty assessment into planning processes
- Use scenario planning for strategic decisions
- Build adaptation checkpoints into project plans

3. Learning and Development

- Include risk efficacy skills in training curricula
- Create internal certifications or badges for decision-quality skills
- Use decision simulations in leadership development

Phase 3: Measurement and Adaptation (Ongoing)

At scale, you can't manage what you don't measure—but you also can't measure everything. The key is measuring the right things.

Scaling Measurement

Research on measurement at scale suggests:

Measure samples, not everything – You don't need decision journals for every decision in a ten-thousand-person organization. Sample strategically.

Use leading indicators – Don't just measure whether practices are being followed (lagging). Measure whether conditions for good decision-making exist (leading): psychological safety, time for deliberation, access to diverse information, etc.

Balance quantitative and qualitative – Quantitative metrics show trends; qualitative stories explain them. You need both.

Measure coherence, not just compliance – Are different parts of the organization implementing risk efficacy in ways that work together? Or are they creating incompatible approaches?

Adaptation Mechanisms

At scale, you need formal mechanisms for learning and adapting:

Regular scaling reviews – Quarterly reviews of what's working and what's not as practices spread

Cross-functional councils – Representatives from different departments sharing lessons and solving coordination problems

Adaptation protocols – Clear processes for customizing practices while maintaining principles

Feedback channels – Ways for people at all levels to report what's working and what's not

The Challenge of Resistance

Resistance isn't a problem to eliminate but a signal to understand. Research on organizational change shows that resistance typically comes in five forms, each requiring different responses (Ford & Ford, *Organizational Dynamics*, 2009):

1. "This won't work here" Resistance

    Signal: People believe their context is unique
    Response: Show how principles apply across contexts while allowing practice customization

2. "This adds bureaucracy" Resistance

    Signal: People feel burdened by new processes
    Response: Simplify, integrate into existing workflows, show time savings from better decisions

3. "This threatens my expertise" Resistance

    Signal: People feel their judgment is being replaced by processes
    Response: Position risk efficacy as enhancing expertise, not replacing it

4. "This conflicts with other priorities" Resistance

Signal: People feel overwhelmed by competing demands
Response: Integrate, don't add. Show how risk efficacy helps achieve existing priorities

5. "I don't know how" Resistance

Signal: People lack skills or understanding
Response: Provide training, coaching, and clear examples

Case Study: Scaling Across a Hospital Network

As an illustrative example, consider how a hospital network would scale risk efficacy from a pilot in one surgical department to a system-wide approach over four years:

Year 1: Pilot (1 department)

- Focus: Complex surgical decisions
- Practices: Decision journals, pre-op uncertainty assessment, calibration tracking
- Results: 40% reduction in complications

Year 2: First wave (3 departments)

- Customized for: Emergency medicine, ICU, cardiology
- Different practices by department: ED focused on rapid calibration, ICU on adaptation, cardiology on uncertainty communication
- Common principles: Process matters, uncertainty acknowledged, calibration tracked
- Results: Varying but positive; learned what customization worked

Year 3: Second wave (12 departments)

- Developed department-specific playbooks
- Created cross-department council for coordination
- Integrated into existing morbidity/mortality reviews
- Results: System-wide complication reduction, but uneven adoption

Year 4: System integration

- Built risk efficacy into: Credentialing, quality metrics, strategic planning
- Created system-level measurement: Decision quality index
- Developed internal certification for decision coaches
- Results: Sustained improvement, cultural shift toward transparency

Key insights from scaling:

- Customization was essential but challenging to manage
- Middle managers were the key scaling agents
- Measurement had to evolve with scale
- Resistance was inevitable but manageable when understood
- Principles held constant while practices varied

The Architecture of Scale
Scaling risk efficacy requires building organizational architecture:

Decision Rights Architecture

Clear maps of who decides what, with what information, under what constraints. Research shows that decision clarity improves both speed and quality (Blenko et al., *Harvard Business Review*, 2010).

Information Architecture

Systems that get the right information to the right people at the right time, in the right form. Not more information—better information flow.

Feedback Architecture

Loops that connect decisions to outcomes, learning to improvement. At scale, these must be designed, not left to chance.

Learning Architecture

Mechanisms for capturing, distributing, and applying lessons about what works in decision-making.

Cultural Architecture

Norms, stories, rituals, and symbols that reinforce risk efficacy principles at scale.

The Long Game

Scaling takes time—typically 3-5 years for meaningful, sustained change. Research on major organizational initiatives shows a consistent pattern: quick wins in year 1, consolidation in year 2, real impact in years 3-5 (Kotter, 1996).

The organizations that succeed at scaling share characteristics:

Strategic patience – They don't expect immediate transformation

Adaptive persistence – They persist with principles while adapting practices

Measurement discipline – They measure what matters and adjust based on data

Leadership continuity – Key leaders stay engaged through the multi-year journey

Learning orientation – They treat scaling as a learning process, not an implementation project

The Scaling Premium

Organizations that successfully scale risk efficacy gain advantages that compound over time:

Decision quality at scale – Not just pockets of excellence but systemic capability

Cultural coherence – Shared understanding of what good decision-making looks like across diverse contexts

Learning velocity – The organization learns faster because decision processes are visible and comparable

Adaptive capacity – The organization can adjust not just individual decisions but decision systems as conditions change

Talent development – People develop decision-making skills that transfer across roles and contexts

Innovation advantage – Better decision-making enables more effective innovation

Risk management – Systematic approach to uncertainty reduces catastrophic risk

Perhaps most importantly, these organizations develop what systems theorists call "requisite variety"—the internal complexity needed to match external complexity (Ashby, *An Introduction to Cybernetics*, 1956). They become as nuanced in their decision-making as the world is in its challenges.

The Way Forward

Scaling is where good ideas become real impact. It's also where good ideas get distorted, diluted, or defeated. The difference between scaling that preserves essence and scaling that loses it isn't luck—it's design.

The risk efficacy framework provides the essence—the core principles of good decision-making. Scaling provides the challenge—how to spread those principles without diluting them, how to adapt practices without losing coherence, how to measure progress without creating bureaucracy.

The organizations that navigate this challenge successfully won't just have better decision-making in some teams. They'll have better decision-making as a organizational capability—a built-in advantage in a world where the quality of decisions determines the quality of outcomes.

The next chapter will explore what comes after scaling: how risk efficacy evolves as organizations master it, how it connects to broader societal systems, and what the future of decision-making might look like in organizations that take these ideas seriously.

Reflection Questions:

- 83. Consider your organization at its current scale. What aspects of risk efficacy would be easiest to scale? What would be hardest?
- 84. Think about resistance you've seen to new initiatives in your organization. What form did it take? How was it handled? What would you do differently?
- 85. If you were to lead scaling of risk efficacy in your organization, where would you start? What would be your first three moves?

Exercise: Scaling Readiness Assessment

Assess your organization's readiness to scale risk efficacy:

- 86. **Decision typology**: What types of decisions does your organization make? Where are they made?
- 87. **Cultural readiness**: Which parts of your organization would embrace risk efficacy? Which would resist? Why?

- 88. **Infrastructure**: What existing systems could support scaling? What would hinder it?
- 89. **Stakeholders**: Who are the key influencers? Innovators? Resistors?
- 90. **Capacity**: Who would lead scaling? What resources would be needed?

Based on your assessment, draft a one-page scaling plan.

Practice: Scaling Simulation

Imagine you need to explain risk efficacy to three different parts of your organization (e.g., engineering, sales, operations). For each:

- How would you explain the core principles?
- What practices would you emphasize?
- What benefits would you highlight?
- What objections might you hear?
- How would you respond?

The goal isn't to create perfect pitches but to practice adapting core ideas to different contexts—the essential skill of scaling.

Chapter 13: The Future of Decision-Making

The Horizon Problem

In the 1950s, a group of psychologists began studying how people think about the future. They discovered something peculiar: when asked to imagine events in the distant future, people's thoughts were abstract, filled with ideals and generalities. But when asked to imagine the same events in the near future, their thoughts became concrete, practical, and riddled with complications (Trope & Liberman, *Psychological Review*, 2003). The researchers called this "temporal construal theory"—the finding that distance changes how we see.

This explains why thinking about the future of decision-making is so difficult. From a distance, we imagine elegant systems, perfect calibration, and wise choices. Up close, we see the messy reality: resistant cultures, imperfect metrics, and human psychology that stubbornly prefers certainty over truth. The challenge is holding both perspectives simultaneously—the distant ideal and the proximate reality, the architecture and the implementation.

This final chapter attempts that balance. We'll explore what decision-making could become if we take the risk efficacy framework seriously—not just in organizations, but as a society. And we'll consider the obstacles that stand between that future and today.

The Research: How Capabilities Evolve

History shows that human capabilities evolve through predictable stages:

Stage 1: Recognition – We notice a problem or opportunity. In decision-making, this stage has largely passed. We know our natural decision processes are flawed. Kahneman and Tversky's work on biases, Tetlock's work on forecasting, Klein's work on naturalistic decision-making—all have made us aware of both our limitations and our potential.

Stage 2: Measurement – We develop ways to measure what matters. This is where we are now with risk efficacy. The framework provides measurement approaches for calibration, informed navigation, resilience, and outcome achievement. But these measurements are still crude, still burdensome, still primarily used by early adopters.

Stage 3: Integration – Measurement becomes seamless, integrated into normal workflows. Think of how pulse oximeters moved from specialized hospital equipment to smartphone apps and fitness trackers. For decision-making, this would mean risk efficacy measures that are automatically captured as we work, providing real-time feedback without extra effort.

Stage 4: Institutionalization – Practices become standard, expected, built into systems. In medicine, handwashing moved from Semmelweis's controversial suggestion to a non-negotiable standard. For decision-making, this would mean risk efficacy becoming as expected in professional contexts as financial accounting or project management.

Stage 5: Internalization – Skills become automatic, intuitive. Think of how literacy moved from a specialized skill to something most people do without conscious effort. For decision-making, this would mean probabilistic thinking, uncertainty acknowledgement, and calibration becoming second nature.

Risk efficacy as a discipline is somewhere between Stages 2 and 3. We have measurement approaches, but they're not yet integrated seamlessly. The future lies in moving through these stages across more domains and contexts.

The Technological Catalysts

Several technological developments could accelerate this evolution:

Artificial Intelligence and Decision Support

Current AI systems often make decisions opaque or reinforce existing biases. But future systems could be designed to enhance human decision-making in risk efficacy-aligned ways:

Calibration assistants – AI that tracks our predictions and outcomes, providing real-time feedback on our confidence-accuracy alignment.

Uncertainty mappers – Systems that automatically identify and quantify uncertainties in complex situations, highlighting what we know, what we don't know, and what we can't know yet.

Alternative generators – Tools that systematically generate and evaluate alternative approaches we might have missed.

Adaptation simulators – Systems that model how different adaptations might play out, helping us choose more intelligently.

Outcome analyzers – Tools that contextualize outcomes, adjusting for risk, time horizons, and external factors.

The key is designing these systems not to replace human judgment but to augment it—to make us better at being human decision-makers rather than turning us into appendages of machines.

Neuroscience Interfaces

Emerging brain-computer interfaces could provide unprecedented insight into decision processes:

Metacognition monitors – Systems that detect when we're overconfident or underconfident based on neural patterns, providing subtle corrections.

Attention directors – Interfaces that help us maintain situational awareness in complex, high-pressure environments.

Cognitive load managers – Systems that detect when we're approaching cognitive overload and suggest breaks or delegation.

Pattern recognition enhancers – Interfaces that help experts recognize subtle patterns they might otherwise miss.

Stress regulators – Systems that monitor stress levels and suggest interventions before stress impairs decision quality.

These technologies raise obvious ethical questions about privacy and autonomy. But used wisely, they could help us overcome biological limitations that have hampered decision-making for millennia.

Collaboration Platforms

Most important decisions are made in groups, yet most decision-support technology focuses on individuals. Future platforms could enhance collective decision-making:

Diversity trackers – Systems that ensure multiple perspectives are considered and that minority views aren't drowned out.

Psychological safety monitors – Tools that detect when people are hesitating to speak up and create safer conditions for dissent.

Process transparency tools – Platforms that make decision rationales visible and searchable across time and organizational boundaries.

Collective calibration systems – Prediction markets and other tools that aggregate diverse judgments into well-calibrated collective forecasts.

Adaptation coordination platforms – Systems that help teams coordinate adaptations and recoveries effectively.

The Educational Transformation

For risk efficacy to become widespread, education must change at every level:

Early Education (K-12)

Current education often rewards certainty and punishes uncertainty. Right answers get As; "I don't know" gets zeros. This trains exactly the wrong instincts for navigating an uncertain world.

Future education could instead teach:

- **Probabilistic thinking** – Math classes that focus on probability and statistics as much as algebra and calculus
- **Scientific mindset** – Science classes that emphasize hypothesis testing, uncertainty quantification, and belief updating
- **Historical decision analysis** – History classes that examine not just what happened, but how decisions were made and what we can learn from them
- **Deliberate practice in uncertainty** – Assignments that require making predictions, tracking outcomes, and learning from mismatches
- **Resilience building** – Projects that require planning for adaptation and recovering from setbacks

Higher Education

Every discipline could integrate decision-quality training:

- **Business schools** teaching calibration and uncertainty navigation alongside finance and marketing
- **Medical schools** making diagnostic reasoning and uncertainty communication core competencies
- **Engineering programs** emphasizing adaptive design and failure analysis

- **Law schools** focusing on probabilistic reasoning and alternative dispute resolution
- **Policy programs** teaching scenario planning and systems thinking
- **All disciplines** incorporating decision journals and calibration practice

Professional Development

Continuing education could maintain and enhance decision skills:

- **Decision skills maintenance** – Regular training to prevent calibration drift, like racing drivers' simulator time
- **Cross-domain learning** – Opportunities to study decision-making in different fields
- **Mentorship networks** – Systems that pair experienced decision-makers with those developing their skills
- **Certification pathways** – Credentials that recognize decision-making expertise
- **Learning communities** – Groups that practice and discuss decision quality together

The Organizational Evolution

As risk efficacy spreads, organizations will evolve in predictable ways:

New Roles and Structures

Decision quality officers – Executives responsible for decision processes across the organization, analogous to chief financial officers for financial processes

Calibration coaches – Professionals who help teams and individuals maintain well-calibrated judgment

Uncertainty navigators – Specialists who help teams identify, quantify, and plan for uncertainties in complex projects

Resilience facilitators – Experts in helping organizations adapt intelligently and recover effectively

Outcome contextualizers – Professionals who help interpret outcomes with appropriate nuance (risk adjustment, time horizons, external factors)

New Metrics and Incentives

Decision quality indices – Composite measures of how well an organization makes decisions, tracked alongside financial metrics

Calibration-based compensation – Bonus systems that reward accurate confidence as much as good outcomes

Promotion by decision quality – Advancement based on demonstrated decision-making skill, not just results or perceived confidence

Learning credits – Recognition for improving decision processes, not just achieving outcomes

Adaptation metrics – Measurement of how well organizations adapt to change and recover from problems

New Cultural Norms

Psychological safety as prerequisite – Recognition that without safety, good decision-making is impossible

Transparency as default – Decision processes and rationales routinely visible across the organization

Uncertainty as respected – Expressing doubt seen as strength, not weakness

Adaptation as expected – Changing course based on new evidence seen as intelligent, not inconsistent

Calibration as valued – Accurate confidence assessment prized over confident presentation

Learning as continuous – Every decision seen as opportunity to improve

The Societal Shift

Beyond organizations, widespread adoption of risk efficacy principles could transform societal systems:

Media and Public Discourse

Calibrated reporting – News that presents probabilities rather than false certainties: "There's a 70% chance the bill will pass" rather than "The bill will pass"

Uncertainty acknowledgement – Reporting that highlights what's unknown rather than pretending everything is clear

Process transparency – Coverage that explains how decisions were made, not just what was decided

Error correction normalization – Media that celebrates updating stories with new information rather than pretending initial reports were complete

Outcome contextualization – Analysis that considers time horizons, external factors, and alternatives when evaluating outcomes

Governance and Policy

Probabilistic policymaking – Policies designed with explicit uncertainty ranges and adaptation triggers

Decision process transparency – Public visibility into how policy decisions are made, with rationale documented

Calibrated leadership – Political leaders who express appropriate confidence rather than false certainty

Adaptive governance – Systems designed to adjust as circumstances change rather than rigidly sticking to plans

Outcome evaluation with nuance – Policy evaluation that considers appropriate timeframes, unintended consequences, and external factors

Professional Standards

Decision quality credentials – Professions requiring demonstrated decision-making skill for licensure or advancement
Error reporting systems – Safe ways for professionals to share mistakes and near-misses for collective learning
Calibration maintenance – Continuing education requirements focused on maintaining decision quality
Cross-professional learning – Systems for sharing decision-making insights across fields
Resilience standards – Professional standards that include adaptation and recovery capability

The Obstacles Ahead

This future won't arrive automatically. Significant obstacles stand in the way:

Psychological Resistance

Our brains prefer certainty to accuracy, simplicity to complexity, speed to deliberation. These preferences are deep-seated, evolved over millennia. Changing them requires not just new systems but new ways of thinking—what psychologist Carol Dweck calls "rewiring" (Dweck, 2006).

Institutional Inertia

Organizations, professions, and societies have tremendous inertia. Existing systems reward existing behaviors. Changing them requires not just better ideas but patient, persistent effort across years or decades.

Measurement Challenges

Many aspects of decision quality are difficult to measure reliably. Without good measurement, improvement is haphazard. Developing valid, reliable, practical measures across diverse contexts remains a significant challenge.

Equity Concerns

Any new system of recognition and reward risks creating new inequities. Unless carefully designed, risk efficacy measurement could advantage those with certain backgrounds or learning styles. Ensuring equitable implementation requires constant vigilance.

Technological Pitfalls

Technology that could enhance decision-making could also undermine it—through surveillance that reduces psychological safety, algorithms that embed bias, or systems that automate away human judgment entirely.

Cultural Resistance

Cultures change slowly. Moving from cultures that value certainty, speed, and confidence to cultures that value calibration, deliberation, and uncertainty navigation requires challenging deeply held beliefs.

The Path Through
Despite these obstacles, the path forward is discernible:

Short term (1-3 years): Spread awareness and build proof points. More organizations pilot risk efficacy approaches. Researchers refine measurement methods. Early adopters share successes and failures. Educational institutions begin incorporating decision quality concepts.

Medium term (3-10 years): Develop infrastructure and standards. Professional associations incorporate decision quality into certifications. Educational institutions develop curricula. Technology platforms integrate decision support tools. More organizations adopt risk efficacy measurement.

Long term (10+ years): Achieve cultural shift. Risk efficacy becomes expected rather than exceptional. Decision quality becomes a standard dimension of organizational and professional assessment. Societal institutions begin adopting principles.

This path isn't inevitable. It requires deliberate effort by many people across many domains. But it's achievable—and worth achieving.

The Ultimate Question

All this raises a fundamental question: What are we optimizing for?

Traditional decision-making systems often optimize for confidence, speed, consistency, and boldness. The risk efficacy framework suggests different optimization targets: calibration, informed navigation, resilience, and contextualized outcome achievement.

But behind these technical dimensions lies a deeper question about values. What kind of decision-makers do we want to be? What kind of organizations do we want to build? What kind of society do we want to create?

The risk efficacy framework, at its heart, represents a set of values:

- **Humility** – Recognizing the limits of our knowledge and judgment
- **Curiosity** – Maintaining interest in what we don't know
- **Courage** – Acting despite uncertainty rather than pretending it doesn't exist

- **Wisdom** – Knowing when to be confident and when to doubt, when to persist and when to adapt
- **Responsibility** – Acknowledging that our decisions affect others and therefore deserve our best thinking
- **Learning** – Treating every decision as an opportunity to improve
- **Fairness** – Recognizing excellence wherever it appears, not just in certain styles

These values aren't new. They're as old as philosophy. What's new is the possibility of building systems that embody them—measurement systems that value calibration, educational systems that teach uncertainty navigation, organizational systems that reward intelligent adaptation, societal systems that contextualize outcomes.

The Choice Before Us

We stand at a peculiar moment in history. Our decisions have never mattered more—climate change, artificial intelligence, global health, economic inequality all require wise choices. And yet our decision-making capabilities have never been so tested—by complexity, by speed, by interdependence.

The gap between the importance of our decisions and our capacity to make them well has never been wider. That gap represents risk, but also opportunity.

We can continue with decision-making as we've always done—relying on intuition, rewarding confidence, celebrating outcomes regardless of process. Or we can choose something different—something more deliberate, more measured, more humble, more wise.

The risk efficacy framework offers one path toward that different approach. It's not the only path, and it's certainly not complete. But it's a start—an attempt to build measurement and improvement systems for one of humanity's most important but least developed capabilities.

The Work Ahead

The work ahead isn't technical, though it has technical dimensions. It isn't organizational, though it must happen in organizations. It isn't even societal, though its implications are societal.

The work ahead is fundamentally human. It's about developing our capacity to think well in the face of uncertainty, to act wisely despite complexity, to learn humbly from both success and failure.

This work won't be completed in our lifetimes. Like all truly important work, it extends beyond any individual or generation. But we can contribute—by practicing risk efficacy in our own decisions, by building systems that support it in our organizations, by teaching its principles to others.

Every decision we make—every time we express calibrated confidence rather than false certainty, every time we acknowledge uncertainty rather than hiding it, every time we adapt intelligently rather than stubbornly persisting, every time we contextualize outcomes rather than taking them at face value—we move the needle. We make the future of decision-making slightly more likely, slightly more real.

And in a world where the quality of our decisions determines the quality of our future, that's work worth doing.

Final Reflection Questions:

- 91. Looking back on your journey through this book, what's the most important insight you've gained about decision-making?
- 92. What one change will you make in your own decision-making as a result?
- 93. What one contribution will you make to improving decision-making in your organization or community?
- 94. Imagine it's twenty years from now. What does good decision-making look like in your field? What role did you play in getting there?

Final Exercise: Your Decision-Making Legacy

Take thirty minutes to write a brief letter to your future self, five years from now. Include:

- 95. How you want your decision-making to have improved over those five years?
- 96. What contributions you want to have made to others' decision-making?
- 97. What systems you want to have helped build or improve?
- 98. What you're willing to commit to now to make that future possible?

Seal the letter and set a calendar reminder to open it in five years. The future of decision-making begins with the decisions we make today.

Epilogue: A Personal Note

I began this book with a question: What does it mean to be good at deciding things? I end it with a realization: We may never fully answer that question, but in trying, we become better at deciding—and better at being human in an uncertain world.

The work continues. The conversation continues. I invite you to join both.

—

The journey of a thousand decisions begins with a single, well-considered choice.

APPENDIX A: RISK EFFICACY ASSESSMENT TOOLS

Simplified worksheets for self-reflection. Professional templates with detailed guidance: riskefficacy.org/implementation.

For career documentation: Submit your decision portfolio at riskefficacy.org/registry to receive an official Risk Efficacy score from our proprietary engine, a detailed assessment report, and optional global leaderboard placement. Official reports can be shared with employers, boards, and stakeholders as Risk EfficacyTM verified evidence of decision-making capability.

A1. Decision Quality Scorecard

Instructions: Use this scorecard for strategic decisions (major investments, key hires, etc.). Complete assessment before deciding.

Scoring Scale:
1 = Major deficiencies
2 = Some deficiencies
3 = Adequate
4 = Good
5 = Excellent

Calibration

Assessment Criteria:

- Confidence level stated (0-100%)
- Reasoning for confidence documented
- Past accuracy considered
- Key evidence for/against noted

APPENDIX A: RISK EFFICACY ASSESSMENT TOOLS — 175

Score: _____
Evidence/Notes:

Post-Decision   Review:

Informed Navigation

Assessment Criteria:

- Diverse sources consulted (minimum 3 types)
- Signal-to-noise ratio assessed
- Key uncertainties explicitly listed
- Conflicting data addressed
- Alternatives considered

Score: _____
Evidence/Notes:

Post-Decision   Review:

Resilience

Assessment Criteria:

- Adaptation triggers defined
- Contingency plans prepared
- Resources allocated for flexibility
- Recovery protocols established

Score: _____
Evidence/Notes:

Post-Decision   Review:

Outcome Achievement

Assessment Criteria:

- Success criteria defined pre-decision
- Timeframes for evaluation specified
- Risk adjustment considered
- External factors accounted for

Score: _____
Evidence/Notes:

Post-Decision Review:

Integration
Assessment Criteria:

- Components balanced appropriately
- Tensions between dimensions managed
- Decision coherent across timeframes
- Stakeholder perspectives integrated

Score: _____
Evidence/Notes:

Post-Decision Review:

Post-Decision Analysis Questions:
1. Decision process quality (1-10): _____
2. Outcome quality (1-10): _____
3. Gap between expected/actual outcome:

4. Key improvement for next time:

A2. Calibration Tracking Worksheet
Weekly Tracking:
Use this format to track each prediction:
Entry 1

APPENDIX A: RISK EFFICACY ASSESSMENT TOOLS

Date: _____
Prediction: _____
Confidence (%): _____
Outcome: _____
Score: _____
Learning: _____

Entry 2
Date: _____
Prediction: _____
Confidence (%): _____
Outcome: _____
Score: _____
Learning: _____

Entry 3
Date: _____
Prediction: _____
Confidence (%): _____
Outcome: _____
Score: _____
Learning: _____

Calibration Score Formula:
Score = 100 - |Confidence - Actual|
(Actual = 100 if correct, 0 if incorrect)

Monthly Analysis:
Average Score: _____
Overconfidence Patterns: _____
Underconfidence Patterns: _____
Improvement Plan: _____

A3. Uncertainty Mapping Template

Uncertainty Inventory:
Use this format for each uncertainty:

Uncertainty 1
Description: _____
Type (Aleatory/Epistemic): _____

Impact (High/Medium/Low): _____
Current Knowledge: _____
Action Plan: _____

Uncertainty 2
Description: _____
Type (Aleatory/Epistemic): _____
Impact (High/Medium/Low): _____
Current Knowledge: _____
Action Plan: _____

Type: Aleatory (random) or Epistemic (knowledge gap)
Impact: High, Medium, Low

Scenario Planning:

Base Case
Probability (%): _____
Key Indicators: _____
Preparedness Actions: _____

Alternative Scenario 1
Probability (%): _____
Key Indicators: _____
Preparedness Actions: _____

Alternative Scenario 2
Probability (%): _____
Key Indicators: _____
Preparedness Actions: _____

Tail Risk Scenario
Probability (%): _____
Key Indicators: _____
Preparedness Actions: _____

A4. Decision Journal Template

Decision Details:
Date: _____
Context: _____
Timeframe: _____
Stakes: _____

Information Considered:
Sources: _____
Key Data: _____
Conflicting Info: _____
Assumptions: _____
Uncertainties:
Known Unknowns: _____
Probabilities: _____
Worst-Case: _____
Alternatives Considered:
1. _____ (Pros: _____, Cons: _____)
2. _____ (Pros: _____, Cons: _____)
3. _____ (Pros: _____, Cons: _____)
Decision & Rationale: _____
Confidence Level: _____%
Reason: _____
Adaptation Plan:
Success Indicators: _____
Failure Indicators: _____
Review Points: _____
Contingency Triggers: _____
Implementation Notes: _____
Post-Decision Review (1-3 months later):
Actual Outcome: _____
Key Differences: _____
Process Strengths: _____
Process Improvements: _____
Learning: _____

A5. Team Decision Assessment Protocol

Pre-Decision Checklist:

- Decision type identified
- Decision rights clarified
- Timeline established

- Stakeholders mapped
- Information needs identified
- Uncertainty assessment completed
- Review process defined

During Decision:

- Multiple alternatives generated
- Probabilistic thinking applied
- Minority opinions heard
- Assumptions challenged
- Confidence calibrated
- Adaptation plan created

Post-Decision Review (within 1 week):
Process Review:
What worked well? _____
What could improve? _____
Calibration adequate? _____
Adaptation appropriate? _____
Outcome Review:
Outcome vs. expectations? _____
Key factors? _____
Role of luck? _____
Learning Capture:
Process improvement: _____
Team insight: _____
Success to celebrate: _____

APPENDIX B: IMPLEMENTATION RESOURCES

B1. 90-Day Implementation Plan

Month 1: Foundation

Week 1-2: Awareness & Assessment

- Conduct current-state decision audit
- Identify pilot team/area
- Train pilot team on basic concepts

Week 3-4: Measurement Setup

- Implement simple decision tracking
- Establish baseline metrics
- Create psychological safety foundation

Month 2: Practice

Week 5-8: Skill Development

- Weekly calibration practice
- Decision journal implementation
- Team decision protocol testing

Week 9: Mid-point Review

- Assess progress
- Adjust approach
- Share early learnings

Month 3: Integration
Week 10-12: System Integration

- Connect to existing processes
- Train additional team members
- Develop internal expertise

Week 13: Evaluation & Planning

- Evaluate pilot results
- Plan next phase
- Document lessons learned

B2. Training Modules Outline

Module 1: Foundations of Risk Efficacy (2 hours)
- The outcome fallacy
- Components of decision quality
- Introduction to measurement

Module 2: Calibration Mastery (3 hours)
- Confidence vs. accuracy
- Prediction tracking
- Calibration improvement techniques

Module 3: Informed Navigation (3 hours)
- Information integration
- Uncertainty handling
- Scenario planning

Module 4: Resilience (2 hours)
- Adaptation planning
- Recovery protocols
- Learning from failure

Module 5: Outcome Achievement (2 hours)
- Contextualizing outcomes
- Time horizon thinking
- Risk adjustment

Module 6: Integration & Application (4 hours)
- Balancing decision components
- Context-based application
- Team decision processes

B3. Communication Templates

Launch Announcement
Subject: Introducing Our Decision Quality Initiative
Key Messages:

- Why decision quality matters for our success
- What risk efficacy means in practice
- How we'll measure and improve
- What's expected of everyone
- Support available

Timeline:

- Pilot phase: [Dates]
- Training schedule: [Details]
- Full implementation: [Target]

Progress Updates
Monthly Update Template:

- What we've implemented
- What we're learning
- Success stories

- Challenges and how we're addressing them
- Next steps
- How to get involved

Recognition Communications
Recognizing Good Decision-Making:

- Describe the decision context
- Highlight the quality decision process used
- Explain why it was effective
- Connect to organizational values
- Encourage others to learn from the example

B4. Integration Checklists

With Performance Management
- [ ] Decision quality metrics in reviews
- [ ] Calibration tracking in development plans
- [ ] Promotion criteria include decision skills
- [ ] Training on giving decision process feedback

With Strategic Planning
- [ ] Uncertainty assessment in planning process
- [ ] Scenario planning for major initiatives
- [ ] Adaptation checkpoints in project plans
- [ ] Decision reviews for strategic choices

With Risk Management
- [ ] Decision quality as risk factor
- [ ] Near-miss reporting for decision processes
- [ ] Learning integration from decision reviews
- [ ] Risk-adjusted decision metrics

With Learning & Development
- [ ] Decision skills in competency models
- [ ] Training curriculum integration
- [ ] Mentorship for decision development
- [ ] Knowledge sharing of decision patterns

APPENDIX C: KEY RESEARCH BY CHAPTER

This appendix highlights the foundational studies and concepts explored in each chapter. It is designed for leaders who wish to delve deeper into the evidence behind the framework. A complete Reference List is provided at the end of the book.

Introduction & Series Introduction

- Anderson et al. (2012): Demonstrates how confidence, not just competence, grants influence in groups, creating systemic bias.
- Lovallo & Kahneman (2003): Explores the "delusion of success"—how optimistic biases undermine executive decisions and strategic planning.
- Kahneman & Tversky (1979): The foundational work on Prospect Theory, explaining how humans deviate from rational choice when judging risk.
- Tetlock & Gardner (2015): Documents the superior, calibrated judgment of "superforecasters," proving that probabilistic thinking can be learned and measured.

Chapter 1: The Measurement Problem

- Baron & Hershey (1988): Landmark study on "outcome bias"—showing people judge decision quality based on results, even when the process is identical.

- Fama & French (2010): Finance study examining whether top fund managers exhibit skill or luck, highlighting the signal-in-noise problem in performance evaluation.
- Weick & Sutcliffe (2007): Research on High-Reliability Organizations (HROs), which institutionalize process-over-outcome thinking to manage extreme risk.

Chapter 2: The Silent Components

- Charness et al. (2001): Chess study showing how expert cognition becomes neurologically efficient and invisible, making it hard to measure.
- Fenton-O'Creevy et al. (2003): Found that the most successful traders excel at "constructive doubt" and information filtering, not just information gathering.
- Brescoll (2012): Research on gender and communication, showing women are more likely to express calibrated uncertainty, which is often misinterpreted as a lack of confidence.

Chapter 3: The Calibration Gap

- Lundeberg et al. (1994): Meta-analysis showing women tend to be better calibrated (confidence matches accuracy) than men, yet are often penalized for it.
- Fleming et al. (2012): Neuroscience research identifying the brain's separate pathways for feelings of certainty and actual knowledge.
- Murphy & Winkler (1977): Classic study on weather forecasters, a profession that excels by measuring and rewarding calibration (accurate probability estimates).

Chapter 4: Informed Navigation

- Bilalić et al. (2011): fMRI study of chess masters, revealing their brain's efficient pattern recognition versus the scattered processing of novices.
- Klein (1998): Introduces "Recognition-Primed Decision Making," describing how experts in fields like firefighting use pattern-matching and mental simulation under pressure.
- Page (2007): Makes the case for cognitive diversity, demonstrating how teams with diverse perspectives and heuristics navigate complexity more effectively.

Chapter 5: Resilience

- Burke et al. (2006): Study of trauma teams showing the highest performance came from "guided adaptability"—modifying protocols to fit the situation, not rigid adherence.
- Dweck (2006): Introduces the "growth mindset," a foundational concept for building resilient individuals and cultures that learn from failure.
- Shenhar & Dvir (2007): Project management research showing that projects with explicit adaptation triggers and flexibility succeed at higher rates.

Chapter 6: Outcome Achievement

- Gompers et al. (2011): Longitudinal study of investors, finding past performance is a poor predictor of future success, highlighting the role of luck.
- Locke & Latham (2002): Comprehensive theory of goal-setting, emphasizing the importance of clear pre-commitment to success criteria for evaluation.
- Heilman & Haynes (2005): Research on attribution bias, showing that identical outcomes are credited more to skill for men and more to luck or external factors for women.

Chapter 7: Integration of Pillars

- March (1991): Seminal paper on the organizational tension between "exploration" (search, innovation) and "exploitation" (refinement, execution), a key integration challenge.
- Weick & Sutcliffe (2007): Further HRO principles like "preoccupation with failure" and "sensitivity to operations" that describe integrated, vigilant decision-making systems.

Chapter 8: From Theory to Practice

- Pfeffer & Sutton (2000): Examines the "knowing-doing gap"—why organizations fail to implement what they know, highlighting cultural and procedural barriers.
- Edmondson (2012): Research on "teaming"—how to build psychological safety and learning behaviors in dynamic, cross-functional teams, critical for implementation.
- Rousseau (2006): Makes the case for "evidence-based management," paralleling the book's call for evidence-based talent decisions.

Chapter 9: Building Measurement Systems

- Pronovost et al. (2006): The landmark Michigan ICU study where measuring and supporting a simple process (checklist for central lines) drastically reduced mortality, showcasing process measurement power.
- Tannenbaum & Cerasoli (2013): Meta-analysis proving that structured team debriefs focusing on process significantly improve future performance.

Chapter 10: Recognizing Merit in Uncertainty

- Correll (2017): Sociological analysis of how gender biases in performance evaluation can be addressed through a "small wins" approach to organizational change.
- Eagly & Johnson (1990): Meta-analysis finding that women's leadership styles are often more participative and less autocratic—styles that may align with informed navigation but are undervalued.

Chapter 11: Cultivating a Culture of Risk Efficacy

- Edmondson (1999): Definitive study establishing "psychological safety" as the critical bedrock for team learning, error admission, and intelligent risk-taking.
- Argyris (1990): Work on "organizational defenses" and how well-intentioned systems can punish honesty and reinforce blind spots.
- Columbia Accident Investigation Board (2003): The official report on the Space Shuttle Columbia disaster, a canonical case study in how cultural "normalization of deviance" leads to catastrophic failure.

Chapter 12: Scaling the Architecture

- Rogers (2003): The classic "Diffusion of Innovations" theory, explaining how new practices spread through different segments of an organization (innovators, early adopters, etc.).
- Nutt (1999): Research finding that half of all organizational decisions fail, often due to poor process and implementation, underscoring the need for scaled systems.

Chapter 13: The Future of Decision-Making

- Kahneman (2011): Synthesizes decades of research on systematic cognitive biases (System 1) and how to engage slower, more analytical thinking (System 2).
- Trope & Liberman (2003): "Temporal Construal Theory" explains why we think abstractly about the distant future but get mired in details for the near term—a key obstacle for long-term decision quality.

APPENDIX D: GLOSSARY OF KEY TERMS

Aleatory Uncertainty: Uncertainty due to randomness or chance that cannot be reduced through additional information or analysis.

Calibration: The degree to which an individual's confidence in their predictions matches the accuracy of those predictions.

Calibration Gap: The discrepancy between expressed confidence and actual accuracy, often manifesting as overconfidence or underconfidence.

Decision Quality: The excellence of the decision-making process, distinct from decision outcome.

Epistemic Uncertainty: Uncertainty due to lack of knowledge that can be reduced through additional information, analysis, or expertise.

Informed Navigation: The process of gathering, filtering, synthesizing, and making sense of diverse information sources while explicitly accounting for uncertainty.

Outcome Fallacy: The erroneous belief that the quality of a decision can be judged solely by its outcome, ignoring the role of luck and process quality.

Psychological Safety: The shared belief that team members can take interpersonal risks without fear of negative consequences.

Resilience: The capacity to execute decisions with both proactive adaptation (planning for flexibility) and effective recovery (responding to surprises).

Risk Efficacy: The measurable capacity to make decisions that create more value than they risk, encompassing calibration, informed navigation, resilience, and contextualized outcome achievement.

Uncertainty Navigation: The systematic approach to acknowledging, quantifying, planning for, and updating based on uncertainties.

APPENDIX E: RECOMMENDED READING & RESOURCES

Foundational Texts

- Kahneman, D. (2011). *Thinking, Fast and Slow*
- Tetlock, P. E., & Gardner, D. (2015). *Superforecasting*
- Klein, G. (1998). *Sources of Power*
- Weick, K. E., & Sutcliffe, K. M. (2007). *Managing the Unexpected*
- Taleb, N. N. (2012). *Antifragile*

Decision Science

- Russo, J. E., & Schoemaker, P. J. (1989). Decision Traps
- Hammond, J. S., Keeney, R. L., & Raiffa, H. (1999). Smart Choices
- Heath, C., & Heath, D. (2013). Decisive

Organizational Learning

- Argyris, C. (1990). Overcoming Organizational Defenses
- Edmondson, A. C. (2012). Teaming
- Senge, P. M. (1990). The Fifth Discipline

Measurement & Implementation

- Meyer, M. W. (1994). Rethinking Performance Measurement
- Pfeffer, J., & Sutton, R. I. (2000). The Knowing-Doing Gap
- Kotter, J. P. (1996). Leading Change

Online Resources

- The Good Judgment Project (superforecasting research)
- Association for Psychological Science (decision science research)
- Society for Judgment and Decision Making
- Harvard Business Review (decision-making articles archive)

Training Programs

- Agency training programs tracking the REDLINE INDEXTM
- Calibration training workshops
- Decision analysis certification programs
- Scenario planning facilitation training
- Adaptive leadership development programs

APPENDIX F: ACKNOWLEDGMENTS

This framework emerged from ten years of observation, experimentation, and synthesis across multiple domains. While the synthesis is original, it stands on the shoulders of researchers and practitioners across fields:

Decision Science: Daniel Kahneman, Amos Tversky, Philip Tetlock, Gary Klein

Organizational Psychology: Amy Edmondson, Karl Weick, Chris Argyris

Neuroscience of Decision-Making: Antonio Damasio, Sarah-Jayne Blakemore

Risk and Uncertainty: Nassim Taleb, Elke Weber, Gerd Gigerenzer

High-Reliability Organizations: Todd LaPorte, Gene Rochlin

Professional Practitioners: The surgeons, traders, racing drivers, and engineers who shared their decision processes and insights

Special thanks to the organizations that pilot early versions of this framework and provide invaluable feedback, and to the teams that continue to refine these ideas in practice.

Contact for Implementation Support: contact@riskefficacy.org

License: This framework is available for organizational implementation with proper attribution. Commercial applications require licensing.

This completes the full manuscript for "Risk Efficacy: Measuring What Matters in High-Stakes Decisions." The book provides both theoretical foundation and practical tools for implementing risk efficacy measurement in or-

ganizations, serving as the foundational volume in The Meritocracy Society Infrastructure Series.

REFERENCE LIST

1. Ambrose, S. E. (1994). *D-Day: June 6, 1944: The climactic battle of World War II*. Simon & Schuster.
2. Anderson, C., Brion, S., Moore, D. A., & Kennedy, J. A. (2012). A status-enhancement account of overconfidence. *Journal of Personality and Social Psychology, 103*(4), 718–735. https://doi.org/10.1037/a0029395
3. Andreassen, P. B. (1990). Judgmental extrapolation and market overreaction: On the use and disuse of news. *Journal of Behavioral Decision Making, 3*(3), 153–174. https://doi.org/10.1002/bdm.3960030303
4. Ansari, S. M., Fiss, P. C., & Zajac, E. J. (2010). Made to fit: How practices vary as they diffuse. *Academy of Management Review, 35*(1), 67–92. https://doi.org/10.5465/amr.35.1.zok67
5. Argyris, C. (1990). *Overcoming organizational defenses: Facilitating organizational learning*. Prentice Hall.
6. Argyris, C., & Schön, D. A. (1978). *Organizational learning: A theory of action perspective*. Addison-Wesley.
7. Armstrong, R. A. (2019). Is there a role for cortisol in the pathophysiology of information overload? *Medical Hypotheses, 122*, 159–162. https://doi.org/10.1016/j.mehy.2018.11.015
8. Ashby, W. R. (1956). *An introduction to cybernetics*. Chapman & Hall.
9. Aston-Jones, G., & Cohen, J. D. (2005). An integrative theory of locus coeruleus-norepinephrine function: Adaptive gain and optimal performance. *Annual Review of Neuroscience, 28*, 403–450. https://doi.org/10.1146/annurev.neuro.28.061604.135709
10. Barber, B. M., & Odean, T. (2001). Boys will be boys: Gender, overconfidence, and common stock investment. *The Quarterly*

Journal of Economics, 116(1), 261–292. https://doi.org/10.1162/003355301556400
11. Baron, J., & Hershey, J. C. (1988). Outcome bias in decision evaluation. *Journal of Personality and Social Psychology, 54*(4), 569–579. https://doi.org/10.1037/0022-3514.54.4.569
12. Baron-Cohen, S. (2003). *The essential difference: The truth about the male and female brain.* Basic Books.
13. Bechara, A., Damasio, H., Tranel, D., & Damasio, A. R. (1997). Deciding advantageously before knowing the advantageous strategy. *Science, 275*(5304), 1293–1295. https://doi.org/10.1126/science.275.5304.1293
14. Berner, E. S., & Graber, M. L. (2008). Overconfidence as a cause of diagnostic error in medicine. *The American Journal of Medicine, 121*(5), S2–S23. https://doi.org/10.1016/j.amjmed.2008.01.001
15. Bilalić, M., Langner, R., Erb, M., & Grodd, W. (2010). Mechanisms and neural basis of object and pattern recognition: A study with chess experts. *Journal of Experimental Psychology: General, 139*(4), 728–742. https://doi.org/10.1037/a0020756
16. Bilalić, M., Langner, R., Erb, M., & Grodd, W. (2011). The role of the temporoparietal junction in the acquisition of complex skills: Evidence from chess experts. *Cerebral Cortex, 21*(12), 2882–2890. https://doi.org/10.1093/cercor/bhr080
17. Birkmeyer, J. D., Stukel, T. A., Siewers, A. E., Goodney, P. P., Wennberg, D. E., & Lucas, F. L. (2003). Surgeon volume and operative mortality in the United States. *New England Journal of Medicine, 349*(22), 2117–2127. https://doi.org/10.1056/NEJMsa035205
18. Blenko, M. W., Mankins, M. C., & Rogers, P. (2010, June). The decision-driven organization. *Harvard Business Review.* https://hbr.org/2010/06/the-decision-driven-organization
19. Boje, D. M. (2001). *Narrative methods for organizational and communication research.* SAGE Publications.

20. Borman, W. C. (1991). Job behavior, performance, and effectiveness. In M. D. Dunnette & L. M. Hough (Eds.), *Handbook of industrial and organizational psychology* (2nd ed., Vol. 2, pp. 271–326). Consulting Psychologists Press.
21. Bornmann, L., & Mutz, R. (2015). Growth rates of modern science: A bibliometric analysis based on the number of publications and cited references. *Journal of the Association for Information Science and Technology, 66*(11), 2215–2222. https://doi.org/10.1002/asi.23329
22. Brescoll, V. L. (2012). Who takes the floor and why: Gender, power, and volubility in organizations. *Administrative Science Quarterly, 57*(4), 622–641. https://doi.org/10.1177/0001839212439994
23. Bruine de Bruin, W., Parker, A. M., & Fischhoff, B. (2007). Individual differences in adult decision-making competence. *Journal of Personality and Social Psychology, 92*(5), 938–956. https://doi.org/10.1037/0022-3514.92.5.938
24. Buckner, R. L., Andrews-Hanna, J. R., & Schacter, D. L. (2008). The brain's default network: Anatomy, function, and relevance to disease. *Annals of the New York Academy of Sciences, 1124*(1), 1–38. https://doi.org/10.1196/annals.1440.011
25. Burke, C. S., Stagl, K. C., Salas, E., Pierce, L., & Kendall, D. (2006). Understanding team adaptation: A conceptual analysis and model. *Journal of Applied Psychology, 91*(6), 1189–1207. https://doi.org/10.1037/0021-9010.91.6.1189
26. Byrnes, J. P., Miller, D. C., & Schafer, W. D. (1999). Gender differences in risk taking: A meta-analysis. *Psychological Bulletin, 125*(3), 367–383. https://doi.org/10.1037/0033-2909.125.3.367
27. Carnahan, S., & Greenwood, B. N. (2018). Managers' political beliefs and gender inequality among subordinates: Does his ideology matter more than hers? *Strategic Management Journal, 39*(3), 596–621. https://doi.org/10.1002/smj.2712
28. Charness, N., Reingold, E. M., Pomplun, M., & Stampe, D. M. (2001). The perceptual aspect of skilled performance in chess:

Evidence from eye movements. *Memory & Cognition, 29*(8), 1146–1152. https://doi.org/10.3758/BF03206384

29. Columbia Accident Investigation Board. (2003). *Report: Volume 1.* Government Printing Office. https://www.nasa.gov/columbia/home/CAIB_Vol1.html

30. Correll, S. J. (2004). Constraints into preferences: Gender, status, and emerging career aspirations. *American Sociological Review, 69*(1), 93–113. https://doi.org/10.1177/000312240406900106

31. Correll, S. J. (2017). SWS 2016 Feminist Lecture: Reducing gender biases in modern workplaces: A small wins approach to organizational change. *Gender & Society, 31*(6), 725–750. https://doi.org/10.1177/0891243217738518

32. Courtney, H., Kirkland, J., & Viguerie, P. (1997, November–December). Strategy under uncertainty. *Harvard Business Review.* https://hbr.org/1997/11/strategy-under-uncertainty

33. Cowley, R. A. (1976). The resuscitation and stabilization of major multiple trauma patients in a trauma center environment. *Clinical Medicine, 83*(1), 14–22.

34. Croskerry, P. (2009). A universal model of diagnostic reasoning. *Academic Medicine, 84*(8), 1022–1028. https://doi.org/10.1097/ACM.0b013e3181ace703

35. Dalio, R. (2017). *Principles: Life and work.* Simon & Schuster.

36. Dawes, R. M. (1988). *Rational choice in an uncertain world.* Harcourt Brace Jovanovich.

37. Diamond, A. (2013). Executive functions. *Annual Review of Psychology, 64,* 135–168. https://doi.org/10.1146/annurev-psych-113011-143750

38. DOMO. (2023). *Data never sleeps 10.0.* https://www.domo.com/learn/data-never-sleeps-10

39. Driskell, J. E., & Johnston, J. H. (1998). Stress exposure training. In J. A. Cannon-Bowers & E. Salas (Eds.), *Making decisions under stress: Implications for individual and team training* (pp. 191–217). American Psychological Association.

40. Dweck, C. S. (2006). *Mindset: The new psychology of success.* Random House.
41. Eagly, A. H., & Johannesen-Schmidt, M. C. (2001). The leadership styles of women and men. *Journal of Social Issues, 57*(4), 781–797. https://doi.org/10.1111/0022-4537.00241
42. Eagly, A. H., & Johnson, B. T. (1990). Gender and leadership style: A meta-analysis. *Psychological Bulletin, 108*(2), 233–256. https://doi.org/10.1037/0033-2909.108.2.233
43. Edmondson, A. C. (1999). Psychological safety and learning behavior in work teams. *Administrative Science Quarterly, 44*(2), 350–383. https://doi.org/10.2307/2666999
44. Edmondson, A. C. (2012). *Teaming: How organizations learn, innovate, and compete in the knowledge economy.* Jossey-Bass.
45. Edmondson, A. C. (2018). *The fearless organization: Creating psychological safety in the workplace for learning, innovation, and growth.* Wiley.
46. Ellis, S., & Davidi, I. (2005). After-event reviews: Drawing lessons from successful and failed experience. *Journal of Applied Psychology, 90*(5), 857–871. https://doi.org/10.1037/0021-9010.90.5.857
47. Ely, R. J., & Thomas, D. A. (2001). Cultural diversity at work: The effects of diversity perspectives on work group processes and outcomes. *Administrative Science Quarterly, 46*(2), 229–273. https://doi.org/10.2307/2667087
48. Ericsson, K. A., Krampe, R. T., & Tesch-Römer, C. (1993). The role of deliberate practice in the acquisition of expert performance. *Psychological Review, 100*(3), 363–406. https://doi.org/10.1037/0033-295X.100.3.363
49. Fama, E. F., & French, K. R. (2010). Luck versus skill in the cross-section of mutual fund returns. *The Journal of Finance, 65*(5), 1915–1947. https://doi.org/10.1111/j.1540-6261.2010.01598.x
50. Fenton-O'Creevy, M., Nicholson, N., Soane, E., & Willman, P. (2003). Trading on illusions: Unrealistic perceptions of con-

trol and trading performance. *Journal of Occupational and Organizational Psychology, 76*(1), 53–68. https://doi.org/10.1348/096317903321208880

51. Fenton-O'Creevy, M., Nicholson, N., Soane, E., & Willman, P. (2011). *Traders: Risks, decisions, and management in financial markets.* Oxford University Press.

52. Fischhoff, B. (1975). Hindsight ≠ foresight: The effect of outcome knowledge on judgment under uncertainty. *Journal of Experimental Psychology: Human Perception and Performance, 1*(3), 288–299. https://doi.org/10.1037/0096-1523.1.3.288

53. Fleming, S. M., Dolan, R. J., & Frith, C. D. (2012). Metacognition: Computation, biology and function. *Philosophical Transactions of the Royal Society B: Biological Sciences, 367*(1594), 1280–1286. https://doi.org/10.1098/rstb.2012.0020

54. Ford, J. D., & Ford, L. W. (2009). Decoding resistance to change. *Harvard Business Review, 87*(4), 99–103. https://hbr.org/2009/04/decoding-resistance-to-change

55. Frederick, S., Loewenstein, G., & O'Donoghue, T. (2002). Time discounting and time preference: A critical review. *Journal of Economic Literature, 40*(2), 351–401. https://doi.org/10.1257/jel.40.2.351

56. Frederick, S., Novemsky, N., Wang, J., Dhar, R., & Nowlis, S. (2009). Opportunity cost neglect. *Journal of Consumer Research, 36*(4), 553–561. https://doi.org/10.1086/599764

57. Galinsky, A. D., Gruenfeld, D. H., & Magee, J. C. (2003). From power to action. *Journal of Personality and Social Psychology, 85*(3), 453–466. https://doi.org/10.1037/0022-3514.85.3.453

58. Garb, H. N. (1998). *Studying the clinician: Judgment research and psychological assessment.* American Psychological Association.

59. Geertz, C. (1973). *The interpretation of cultures: Selected essays.* Basic Books.

60. Gobet, F., & Charness, N. (2006). Expertise in chess. In K. A. Ericsson, N. Charness, P. J. Feltovich, & R. R. Hoffman (Eds.),

The Cambridge handbook of expertise and expert performance (pp. 523–538). Cambridge University Press.

61. Goldin, C., & Rouse, C. (2000). Orchestrating impartiality: The impact of "blind" auditions on female musicians. *American Economic Review, 90*(4), 715–741. https://doi.org/10.1257/aer.90.4.715

62. Gompers, P. A., Kovner, A., Lerner, J., & Scharfstein, D. S. (2011). Performance persistence in entrepreneurship. *Journal of Financial Economics, 96*(1), 18–32. https://doi.org/10.1016/j.jfineco.2009.11.001

63. Greenspan, A. (2008, October 23). *Testimony before the House Committee on Oversight and Government Reform.* https://www.federalreserve.gov/newsevents/testimony/greenspan20081023a.htm

64. Greenwald, A. G., & Banaji, M. R. (1995). Implicit social cognition: Attitudes, self-esteem, and stereotypes. *Psychological Review, 102*(1), 4–27. https://doi.org/10.1037/0033-295X.102.1.4

65. Hammond, J. S., Keeney, R. L., & Raiffa, H. (1999). *Smart choices: A practical guide to making better decisions.* Harvard Business Review Press.

66. Hatano, G., & Inagaki, K. (1986). Two courses of expertise. In H. Stevenson, H. Azuma, & K. Hakuta (Eds.), *Child development and education in Japan* (pp. 262–272). W. H. Freeman.

67. Heilman, M. E., & Haynes, M. C. (2005). No credit where credit is due: Attributional rationalization of women's success in male-female teams. *Journal of Applied Psychology, 90*(5), 905–916. https://doi.org/10.1037/0021-9010.90.5.905

68. Hollenbeck, J. R., Ilgen, D. R., Sego, D. J., Hedlund, J., Major, D. A., & Phillips, J. (1995). Multilevel theory of team decision making: Decision performance in teams incorporating distributed expertise. *Journal of Applied Psychology, 80*(2), 292–316. https://doi.org/10.1037/0021-9010.80.2.292

69. Holling, C. S. (1973). Resilience and stability of ecological systems. *Annual Review of Ecology and Systematics, 4*(1), 1–23. https://doi.org/10.1146/annurev.es.04.110173.000245
70. Kahneman, D. (2011). *Thinking, fast and slow*. Farrar, Straus and Giroux.
71. Kahneman, D., & Tversky, A. (1979). Prospect theory: An analysis of decision under risk. *Econometrica, 47*(2), 263–291. https://doi.org/10.2307/1914185
72. Kaiser, R. B., Hogan, R., & Craig, S. B. (2008). Leadership and the fate of organizations. *American Psychologist, 63*(2), 96–110. https://doi.org/10.1037/0003-066X.63.2.96
73. Kaplan, R. S., & Norton, D. P. (1996). *The balanced scorecard: Translating strategy into action*. Harvard Business School Press.
74. Keller, T., & Tergan, S.-O. (Eds.). (2005). *Knowledge and information visualization: Searching for synergies*. Springer.
75. Kerr, S. (1975). On the folly of rewarding A, while hoping for B. *Academy of Management Journal, 18*(4), 769–783. https://doi.org/10.5465/255378
76. Klein, G. (1998). *Sources of power: How people make decisions*. MIT Press.
77. Klein, G. (2003). *The power of intuition: How to use your gut feelings to make better decisions at work*. Currency.
78. Klein, G. (2007). Performing a project premortem. *Harvard Business Review, 85*(9), 18–19. https://hbr.org/2007/09/performing-a-project-premortem
79. Klein, G. (2009). *Streetlights and shadows: Searching for the keys to adaptive decision making*. MIT Press.
80. Klein, G. (2013). *Seeing what others don't: The remarkable ways we gain insights*. PublicAffairs.
81. Klein, G. A., Calderwood, R., & Macgregor, D. (1995). Critical decision method for eliciting knowledge. *IEEE Transactions on Systems, Man, and Cybernetics, 19*(3), 462–472. https://doi.org/10.1109/21.31053

82. Koriat, A., Lichtenstein, S., & Fischhoff, B. (1980). Reasons for confidence. *Journal of Experimental Psychology: Human Learning and Memory, 6*(2), 107–118. https://doi.org/10.1037/0278-7393.6.2.107
83. Kotter, J. P. (1996). *Leading change*. Harvard Business School Press.
84. Kuhnen, C. M., & Knutson, B. (2005). The neural basis of financial risk taking. *Neuron, 47*(5), 763–770. https://doi.org/10.1016/j.neuron.2005.08.008
85. Kundel, H. L., Nodine, C. F., Conant, E. F., & Weinstein, S. P. (2007). Holistic component of image perception in mammogram interpretation: Gaze-tracking study. *Radiology, 242*(2), 396–402. https://doi.org/10.1148/radiol.2422051997
86. Lak, A., Costa, G. M., Romberg, E., Koulakov, A. A., Mainen, Z. F., & Kepecs, A. (2014). Orbitofrontal cortex is required for optimal waiting based on decision confidence. *Neuron, 84*(1), 190–201. https://doi.org/10.1016/j.neuron.2014.08.039
87. Laverty, K. J. (1996). Economic "short-termism": The debate, the unresolved issues, and the implications for management practice and research. *Academy of Management Review, 21*(3), 825–860. https://doi.org/10.5465/amr.1996.9702100316
88. Levitin, D. J. (2014). *The organized mind: Thinking straight in the age of information overload*. Dutton.
89. Locke, E. A., & Latham, G. P. (2002). Building a practically useful theory of goal setting and task motivation: A 35-year odyssey. *American Psychologist, 57*(9), 705–717. https://doi.org/10.1037/0003-066X.57.9.705
90. Lovallo, D., & Kahneman, D. (2003). Delusions of success: How optimism undermines executives' decisions. *Harvard Business Review, 81*(7), 56–63. https://hbr.org/2003/07/delusions-of-success
91. Lundeberg, M. A., Fox, P. W., & Punćcohaŕ, J. (1994). Highly confident but wrong: Gender differences and similarities in

confidence judgments. *Journal of Educational Psychology, 86*(1), 114–121. https://doi.org/10.1037/0022-0663.86.1.114

92. Mahoney, M. J. (1977). Publication prejudices: An experimental study of confirmatory bias in the peer review system. *Cognitive Therapy and Research, 1*(2), 161–175. https://doi.org/10.1007/BF01173636

93. Malhotra, N. K. (1982). Information load and consumer decision making. *Journal of Consumer Research, 8*(4), 419–430. https://doi.org/10.1086/208882

94. Malkiel, B. G. (1973). *A random walk down Wall Street*. W. W. Norton & Company.

95. March, J. G. (1991). Exploration and exploitation in organizational learning. *Organization Science, 2*(1), 71–87. https://doi.org/10.1287/orsc.2.1.71

96. March, J. G., & Shapira, Z. (1992). Variable risk preferences and the focus of attention. *Psychological Review, 99*(1), 172–183. https://doi.org/10.1037/0033-295X.99.1.172

97. March, J. G., & Sutton, R. I. (1997). Organizational performance as a dependent variable. *Organization Science, 8*(6), 698–706. https://doi.org/10.1287/orsc.8.6.698

98. May, R. M. (1973). *Stability and complexity in model ecosystems*. Princeton University Press.

99. Mellers, B., Ungar, L., Baron, J., Ramos, J., Gurcay, B., Fincher, K., Scott, S. E., Moore, D., Atanasov, P., Swift, S. A., Murray, T., Stone, E., & Tetlock, P. E. (2014). Psychological strategies for winning a geopolitical forecasting tournament. *Psychological Science, 25*(5), 1106–1115. https://doi.org/10.1177/0956797614524255

100. Merton, R. K. (1948). The self-fulfilling prophecy. The Antioch Review, 8(2), 193–210. https://doi.org/10.2307/4609267

101. Meyer, M. W. (1994, May–June). Rethinking performance measurement. Harvard Business Review. https://hbr.org/1994/05/rethinking-performance-measurement

102. Meyers-Levy, J., & Maheswaran, D. (1991). Exploring differences in males' and females' processing strategies. *Journal of Consumer Research, 18*(1), 63–70. https://doi.org/10.1086/209241
103. Miller, D. T., & Ross, M. (1975). Self-serving biases in the attribution of causality: Fact or fiction? *Psychological Bulletin, 82*(2), 213–225. https://doi.org/10.1037/h0076486
104. Murphy, A. H., & Winkler, R. L. (1977). Reliability of subjective probability forecasts of precipitation and temperature. *Applied Statistics, 26*(1), 41–47. https://doi.org/10.2307/2346866
105. Murphy, K. R., & Cleveland, J. N. (1995). *Understanding performance appraisal: Social, organizational, and goal-based perspectives*. SAGE Publications.
106. Muthukrishnan, A. V., & Wathieu, L. (2007). Superfluous choices and the persistence of preference. *Journal of Consumer Research, 34*(2), 154–160. https://doi.org/10.1086/519142
107. Nemeth, C. J. (1986). Differential contributions of majority and minority influence. *Psychological Review, 93*(1), 23–32. https://doi.org/10.1037/0033-295X.93.1.23
108. Norman, D. A. (1988). *The psychology of everyday things*. Basic Books.
109. Norman, G. R. (2005). Research in clinical reasoning: Past history and current trends. *Medical Education, 39*(4), 418–427. https://doi.org/10.1111/j.1365-2929.2005.02127.x
110. Norman, G. R., Brooks, L. R., & Allen, S. W. (2007). Recall by expert medical practitioners and novices as a record of processing attention. *Journal of Experimental Psychology: Learning, Memory, and Cognition, 33*(2), 461–473. https://doi.org/10.1037/0278-7393.33.2.461
111. Nutt, P. C. (1999). Surprising but true: Half the decisions in organizations fail. *Academy of Management Perspectives, 13*(4), 75–90. https://doi.org/10.5465/ame.1999.2570556
112. Nutt, P. C. (2002). *Why decisions fail: Avoiding the blunders and traps that lead to debacles*. Berrett-Koehler Publishers.

113. O'Reilly, C. A., III. (1980). Individuals and information overload in organizations: Is more necessarily better? *Academy of Management Journal, 23*(4), 684–696. https://doi.org/10.5465/255556
114. Page, S. E. (2007). *The difference: How the power of diversity creates better groups, firms, schools, and societies.* Princeton University Press.
115. Page, S. E. (2017). *The diversity bonus: How great teams pay off in the knowledge economy.* Princeton University Press.
116. Pariser, E. (2011). *The filter bubble: How the new personalized web is changing what we read and how we think.* Penguin Books.
117. Perrow, C. (1984). *Normal accidents: Living with high-risk technologies.* Basic Books.
118. Perry, D. E., Porter, A. A., & Votta, L. G. (2001). Empirical studies of software engineering: A roadmap. In *Proceedings of the Conference on The Future of Software Engineering* (pp. 345–355). Association for Computing Machinery. https://doi.org/10.1145/336512.336586
119. Pfeffer, J., & Sutton, R. I. (2000). *The knowing-doing gap: How smart companies turn knowledge into action.* Harvard Business School Press.
120. Powell, M., & Ansic, D. (1997). Gender differences in risk behaviour in financial decision-making: An experimental analysis. *Journal of Economic Psychology, 18*(6), 605–628. https://doi.org/10.1016/S0167-4870(97)00026-3
121. Pronovost, P., Needham, D., Berenholtz, S., Sinopoli, D., Chu, H., Cosgrove, S., Sexton, B., Hyzy, R., Welsh, R., Roth, G., Bander, J., Kepros, J., & Goeschel, C. (2006). An intervention to decrease catheter-related bloodstream infections in the ICU. *New England Journal of Medicine, 355*(26), 2725–2732. https://doi.org/10.1056/NEJMoa061115
122. Radicati Group. (2023). *Email statistics report, 2023-2027.* https://www.radicati.com/wp/wp-content/uploads/2023/04/Email_Statistics_Report_2023-2027_Executive_Summary.pdf

123. Repenning, N. P., & Sterman, J. D. (2002). Capability traps and self-confirming attribution errors in the dynamics of process improvement. *Administrative Science Quarterly, 47*(2), 265–295. https://doi.org/10.2307/3094806
124. Ridgeway, C. L. (2014). Why status matters for inequality. *American Sociological Review, 79*(1), 1–16. https://doi.org/10.1177/0003122413515997
125. Roberts, K. H. (1993). *New challenges to understanding organizations*. Macmillan.
126. Rogers, E. M. (2003). *Diffusion of innovations* (5th ed.). Free Press.
127. Roese, N. J. (1997). Counterfactual thinking. *Psychological Bulletin, 121*(1), 133–148. https://doi.org/10.1037/0033-2909.121.1.133
128. Ross, L. (1977). The intuitive psychologist and his shortcomings: Distortions in the attribution process. In L. Berkowitz (Ed.), *Advances in experimental social psychology* (Vol. 10, pp. 173–220). Academic Press.
129. Rousseau, D. M. (2006). Is there such a thing as "evidence-based management"? *Academy of Management Review, 31*(2), 256–269. https://doi.org/10.5465/amr.2006.20208679
130. Russo, J. E., & Schoemaker, P. J. H. (1989). *Decision traps: The ten barriers to brilliant decision-making and how to overcome them*. Doubleday.
131. Schein, E. H. (2010). *Organizational culture and leadership* (4th ed.). Jossey-Bass.
132. Schoemaker, P. J. H. (1995). Scenario planning: A tool for strategic thinking. *Sloan Management Review, 36*(2), 25–40.
133. Shenhar, A. J., & Dvir, D. (2007). Project management research: The challenge and opportunity. *Project Management Journal, 38*(2), 93–99. https://doi.org/10.1177/875697280703800210

134. Simons, R. (1995, March–April). Control in an age of empowerment. *Harvard Business Review.* https://hbr.org/1995/03/control-in-an-age-of-empowerment
135. Sterman, J. D. (2000). *Business dynamics: Systems thinking and modeling for a complex world.* Irwin/McGraw-Hill.
136. Surowiecki, J. (2004). *The wisdom of crowds: Why the many are smarter than the few and how collective wisdom shapes business, economies, societies, and nations.* Doubleday.
137. Tamuz, M., & Harrison, M. I. (2006). Improving patient safety in hospitals: Contributions of high-reliability theory and normal accident theory. *Health Services Research, 41*(4p2), 1654–1676. https://doi.org/10.1111/j.1475-6773.2006.00570.x
138. Tannenbaum, S. I., & Cerasoli, C. P. (2013). Do team and individual debriefs enhance performance? A meta-analysis. *Human Factors, 55*(1), 231–245. https://doi.org/10.1177/0018720812448394
139. Tetlock, P. E. (2005). *Expert political judgment: How good is it? How can we know?* Princeton University Press.
140. Tetlock, P. E., & Gardner, D. (2015). *Superforecasting: The art and science of prediction.* Crown Publishers.
141. Thaler, R. H. (1992). *The winner's curse: Paradoxes and anomalies of economic life.* Free Press.
142. Tobar, H. (2014). *Deep down dark: The untold stories of 33 men buried in a Chilean mine, and the miracle that set them free.* Farrar, Straus and Giroux.
143. Trope, Y., & Liberman, N. (2003). Temporal construal. *Psychological Review, 110*(3), 403–421. https://doi.org/10.1037/0033-295X.110.3.403
144. U.S. Department of Defense. (2016). *Red teaming: Guide to alternative analysis techniques.* https://www.hsdl.org/?view&did=804016
145. Weick, K. E., & Sutcliffe, K. M. (2007). *Managing the unexpected: Resilient performance in an age of uncertainty* (2nd ed.). Jossey-Bass.

146. Wolfers, J., & Zitzewitz, E. (2004). Prediction markets. *Journal of Economic Perspectives, 18*(2), 107–126. https://doi.org/10.1257/0895330041371321
147. Woolley, A. W., Chabris, C. F., Pentland, A., Hashmi, N., & Malone, T. W. (2010). Evidence for a collective intelligence factor in the performance of human groups. *Science, 330*(6004), 686–688. https://doi.org/10.1126/science.1193147

Alia Wu is an applied cognitive scientist and founder of Risk Efficacy. Her work spans clinical neuroscience, quantitative finance, and professional motorsport. She studies how people calibrate confidence, gather information, and adapt under uncertainty, and she builds measurement systems for decision quality in high stakes environments. Wu is also the founder of Redline Rising, a nonprofit research and training platform focused on agency training and measurement.

www.ingramcontent.com/pod-product-compliance
Lightning Source LLC
Chambersburg PA
CBHW070621030426
42337CB00020B/3874